THE RUSSIANS

First double page
The small village of Suzdal, northeast of Moscow, has a glorious history. A kremlin (fortress) built during the twelfth century by the princes of Rostov-Suzdal and the Cathedral of the Nativity of the Mother of God, now a museum, still stand.

Second double page
The gilded onion domes of the Church of Saint Sophia in Vologda, a city situated on the bend of a river north of Moscow. The washer-woman and changing sky make this a classic picture of the Russian landscape.

Third double page
A view of the famous Pechory monastery near Pskov, one of the oldest in Russia, which was built in the hollow of a valley rather than on a hillside like most.

Fourth double page
Sichov and his wife, Aïda, at home among paintings from an exhibit they had organized. On the extreme right sits Elena Kozleva, the right hand of Klebanov, the founder of the first free trade union of Soviet workers. The union was dissolved and Klebanov arrested.

Vladimir Sichov

Vladimir Sichov was born in Kazan, in the Soviet Union, in 1945. After earning a degree in radio engineering, he served for two years in the army at Baykonur Cosmodrome, the Soviet space center. After his discharge as a lieutenant in 1971, he worked as a free-lance photographer, shooting souvenir photos and record jackets. He took some 180,000 photographs of his own during this time, and was able to smuggle 5,000 rolls of film out of the Soviet Union to contacts in the West before he emigrated with his family in October 1979. Though both Sichov and his wife Aïda are Orthodox Christians, they secured Jewish visas by inventing relatives in Israel.

The Russians

PHOTOGRAPHS BY *Vladimir Sichov*

TEXT BY EUGENE SILIANOFF

TRANSLATED FROM THE FRENCH

BY ROBERT VOLLRATH

LITTLE, BROWN AND COMPANY   BOSTON   TORONTO

Contents

Chapter 1

Homo Sovieticus Thinks Mostly about Having a Car

The Russian writer Aleksandr Zinoviev calls Kremlinology a pseudoscience. A totally new discipline in France, it offers a wide choice of interpretations about the nature of the Moscow regime and of Russia's political evolution. The two major schools agree about the system's problems and about its totalitarianism, but they disagree about the more deep-seated causes involved. For numerous Marxists and disappointed Communists, today's problems are the result of a misinterpretation, or a perversion, of Lenin's designs for Russia. Stalin and his crimes, then, the euphemistically designated "personality cult," shaped the present regime. Trotsky believed this early on, as the title of his work, *The Revolution Betrayed,* suggests. The system established by the Bolsheviks, even though "betrayed" by Stalin, remained socialist. Many neo-Marxists attempt to blame the evolution of the system into dictatorship half on Stalin's nature and half on a series of circumstances that existed during the first month of the Revolution: civil war, encirclement by unfriendly powers, insurmountable economic difficulties, two ruinous famines, et cetera. Those who defend this thesis do not have an answer to one crucial question: if one does admit that this explanation is true for the beginning of the revolutionary era and during Stalin's time, why does totalitarianism persist today, sixty-three years after October 1917, more than one quarter of a century after the death of Stalin? This leads us to our second theory, generally called the continuity theory. Those who support it, among whom are numerous historians, attribute the system's problems to causes deeply rooted in Russia's long past. The seeds of destruction were planted in the Middle Ages when the Russian state, omnipotent and oppressive, totalitarian before its time, began to expect complete submission of the people's individual and collective existence to the prince's will. Today's totalitarian state is part of a long autocratic tradition. The celebrated book by the Marquis de Custine depicts an Old Russia whose resemblance to the Soviet Union is astounding: the internal passport, the prohibitions and other difficulties involved in traveling to foreign countries, from which the subjects of the Czar return with "as much regret as they had joy in leaving him," "the fanatic submission." The Russia

that the French aristocrat, a convinced royalist championing the cause of the *ancien régime,* found upon arrival was a society where "no happiness is possible because there is no liberty, and which is condemned to widespread deceit; for to speak the truth would be to cause the government to be overthrown . . . , the regime could not stand up to twenty years of free contact with the outside. . . ." It is a prophetic book, read with constant astonishment; it is the description of the Soviet Union of today.

But Custine's book is relatively recent and, for supporters of the "continuity school," we need to go much farther back in history. During the thirteenth, fourteenth, and fifteenth centuries, the somber period of Mongol domination, many of the principalities comprising the remains of the Kiev state were brought under submission. The Mongol (or Tatar) domination lasted for more than two centuries and profoundly affected the Russian nation. The first united Russian government, established by the princes of Moscow, had at its head the Grand Duke Ivan Kalita ("the Moneybag"), who was entirely under Mongol sway. According to the historian Tibor Szamuely, whose family were active in the abortive Hungarian revolution of 1919, these various princes and noblemen, cruelly treated by their Mongol suzerains, applied the same oppressive methods to their own subjects once they were free of the Tatar yoke. Ivan the Terrible, Catherine, Peter the Great, and finally Stalin, according to the continuity theory, simply perpetuated this Russian "tradition." The Soviets have amplified its vices in the twentieth century, but have not essentially changed its nature, deeply anchored in the Russian past.

It isn't a matter of choosing between these two opposing schools. In fact, neither of them finds fault with the Russian people, but rather with their present and former leaders, who have been convinced that the individual must always be sacrificed to the state. As for Vladimir Sichov, he was certainly not preoccupied by these analyses while preparing the admirable photographs of the men and women of his country.

*   *   *

At the dawn of the October Revolution of 1917, Lenin and his companions planned first of all to establish Soviet power and the dictatorship of the proletariat. (This proletariat, incidentally, was next to nonexistent in Russia at the time. There were 2,500,000 industrial workers in 1917, but this figure was severely reduced by the serious problems of the first years immediately following the Revolution.) As soon as these fundamental tasks of the Revolution had been accomplished, a new Soviet man was to emerge, who would be radically different from the men who had grown up under the harsh restraints of capitalistic exploitation. Descriptions of the future *Homo sovieticus,* the living incarnation of socialism triumphant, filled the writings of the first theoreticians of Bolshevism. Builder of a radiant future, this was to be a new man wielding his hammer in a factory that was now his own, swinging a sickle in a countryside freed from serfdom. The Soviet citizen would belong to a new race for which only ideals would count and which would disdain the old incentives of money, profit, and material goods.

Beyond the euphoric promise that accompanied the birth of a new world, however, the new Soviet citizen was left with little. The goods expropriated from the nobility had been liquidated at once, and shortages close to famine made money practically worthless. According to the Greek ex-Communist Kostas Papaioannou, workers' salaries had diminished to a tenth of their 1913 level and were paid in kind.

All that was supposed to come quickly to an end, though, as Soviet man, realizing his own strengths through the Bolshevik regime's nurturing, would begin to build a new society. The state was to "wither"; other constraints were to disappear. The economist Nikolai Bukharin explained that in Communist society, the cruel division of labor that oppresses workers under capitalism would no longer exist. Each would be in his turn engineer, foreman, and, of course, state official, fulfilling each function with the same enthusiasm and competency, and for the same payment. However modest this payment might be, each would cheerfully be content as the state would provide for all his needs: housing, transportation, recreation, entertainment. In *State and Revolution* (1917), Lenin himself proclaims that the "very simple" jobs of former civil servants would now be within reach of the common citizen, who could carry them out quite capably at "workers' salaries." These dreams persisted for a long time. In 1960 the economist Strumilin wrote in his celebrated *Thoughts on the Future* that "each worker can become not only a master in his specialty or even a champion in his favorite sport, but also an inventor, an artist, or a scholar."

In 1924, at the height of his brief legal career, Trotsky sketched a lyrical portrait of man in the Communist future: "[He] will be capable of changing the course of rivers and moving mountains, of building palaces upon the peaks of Mount Blanc or on the Atlantic floor. This man will know how to make his daily life not only rich, colorful, and intense, but also dynamic . . . and will raise himself to an unequaled level to create a higher sociobiological being, a superman. . . . This man will be incomparably stronger, more intelligent, more refined. His body will be more harmonious, his movements more rhythmic, his voice more musical. . . . The average man will rise to the level of an Aristotle, a Goethe, a Marx. . . ." One may ask oneself whether these photographs by Vladimir Sichov bring us confirmation of this sublime vision.

How does Soviet man appear today, in a country where "socialism truly exists," to use the expression of the East German dissident Rudolf Bahro?

Without being reproached with systematic anticommunism, one can agree, looking over evidence that originates in Communist sources, that Soviet man is becoming more and more like any other middle-class citizen of a bourgeois country, and that the ideals proclaimed at the beginning of the revolutionary era have been replaced by a thirst for material goods, a thirst that intensifies as the goods become more inaccessible. If he has obtained decent housing, the dream of the average Soviet citizen is to own an automobile and a *dacha.* In a journal from one of the Eastern bloc countries, an article entitled "The Three Keys" showed the way to material goods. Above the title appears an illustration of three keys on a chain: one for the apartment, one for the car, and one for the country house.

Private cars are still rare in the USSR. The major part of automobile production is destined for export, to ensure the balance of payments. Much of the remaining stock is designated for official use. It is only after the needs of countless bureaucratic agencies of the Party and the government are met that any surplus is available to private citizens. The cost of an automobile is usually twice that of a similar Western model, if one calculates the price at the quoted exchange rate of the ruble. If one considers the work time needed to earn this amount, or if one uses the black market exchange rate, the resulting real price is substantially higher.

The calculation figured in work-hours is the most instructive. The average monthly salary in the Soviet Union is 120 rubles. The Moskvich, the most popular model because it is the easiest to come by and better made than the less expensive Zaporozhetz, has a price tag equal to four years' pay. With salaries ranging from 60 rubles a month ($94) — corresponding to the minimum wage — to 100 or 120 rubles ($156 to $188) for a beginning engineer to 150 rubles ($234) for a salary that is considered satisfactory, it is not only a financial struggle to purchase a car but also a physical one to sign up on the waiting list.

Leaving out of consideration those people who, in the USSR as elsewhere, seem mysteriously to come by incomes that are larger than their declared salaries, the explanation is that there is a type of car-owning family, in spite of modest incomes: these are families in which both husband and wife work, live with their retired parents (who nevertheless go on doing small amounts of business on the black market), and usually have only one child.

For the Moskvich, the buyer must wait at least two years, unless he has connections that can help him. How can this irresistible attraction to the automobile in the Soviet sphere be explained? A car is desirable, just as it is for any Westerner, because it provides access to escape and adventure. For the Soviet citizen, however, the force of this attraction is multiplied, because he has no other way to get away. Entertainment is rare and authorizations for foreign travel, once prohibited altogether, still

only trickle down. Furthermore, a car is desirable because it is rare: there exist only five cars for every thousand inhabitants. Anyone who has a car, either privately or through his employment, would appear very privileged, which, in fact, he is. Ownership of a Moskvich indicates not only financial success, but also an elite affiliation.

There is a passage in Nina and Jean Kehayan's *Red Proletariat Street,* which sums up these long developments. The authors, as youths, were loyal Communists and members of the French Communist Party. Georges Marchais, the head of the French Party, helped them get positions in the foreign language section of the Soviet propaganda service. They spoke Russian and lived, not like other foreigners, but in houses like their colleagues', with their children attending the same neighborhood schools. They perceived very quickly that to emphasize their Party membership immediately put a damper on conversation, incurred a sudden reserve. As they came to know their colleagues better, they realized that "outside official meetings, Soviet comrades could not comprehend that one could be a member of the Communist Party in a detached way in a country like France, where one can have everything, where one can own a private car at the age of thirty."

In 1959, at the height of his power, Nikita Khrushchev had announced, to the applause of the Twenty-first Party Congress, that, based on statistical indices, the standard of living in the USSR would surpass that of the United States by 1970. Khrushchev was removed from the political arena in 1963, only one year after Kremlin-watchers had written that he was more firmly entrenched than ever. Nikita Sergeyevich wasn't around to critique his own prediction and his successors were subsequently wise enough never to repeat his mistake. But the jovial Ukrainian had also made another proclamation: announcing the coming of a global Communist society — which was to occur by the beginning of the 1980s — he described the essential qualities of the Communist man of the future. An official document of the Central Committee specified these qualities in *Pravda* of 10 January 1960: this new man would most notably possess Communist habits and morals. He would have erased from his mind all traces of his capitalistic past. The creation of this new being was to be "one of the principal objectives of the Party's practical work."

It is clear that sixty years have not been enough to create the new Soviet man. The best proof is the fact that official propaganda no longer speaks about him. The Soviet people seem to have preferred their well-being and the realization of their personal ambitions to the triumph of an ideology and the victory of worldwide Communism. At first glance, this would be reassuring to a Western world threatened by Communist ideology: since the Soviet citizen prefers his comfort and because his position has improved to a relative degree, couldn't the Soviet Union be expected to stay on this path and abandon the goal of world conquest?

This question can be answered in two ways. Although it appears that the Soviet people are moving away from Communist ideology, it does not seem that their leaders' imperialist and nationalist tendencies have lost any of their fervor. This nationalism is all the more alarming because it springs from an aggressive tradition that inspires a Russian people obscurely convinced that they have been destined — yesterday by God and today by History — to accomplish a great mission. I was talking recently to a Russian dissident who had just arrived in the West. I mentioned Nikita Khrushchev's ominous prediction: "We will bury you!" I thought I had made him laugh, for his face lit up: "Of course we'll bury you!" His response has two aspects: the anger of all emigrants from the East toward what they call "our lack of backbone; our readiness to kneel down at Brezhnev's slightest frown," and also the conviction that the Russians are our superiors in having the courage to accept the risks and sacrifices that our tastes for comfort have denied us.

A school of thought existed in the fifties, most notably in America, which believed that the gradual improvement in living conditions in the Soviet Union would compel its people to demand more and more comfort and, subsequently, freedom from its leaders, who would in turn grant it, creating a climate hospitable to détente. The economic counterpart to this theory advocates the promotion of East-West trade relations. David Floyd, a longtime Moscow correspondent, wondered in 1969 if, on the contrary, more personal liberty and comfort combined with such a clearly autocratic political system did not represent a greater danger to world peace. He

pointed out that the system of abuse and inefficiency that produced the state of near-famine the Soviets suffered during the first twenty years of the Bolshevik regime also caused hundreds of thousands of soldiers to lay down their arms in front of Hitler. David Floyd was already thinking that it would not be impossible for Stalin's successors to earn their people's allegiance by better satisfying their material needs.

In a recent interview, Aleksandr Zinoviev echoed Floyd's remarks: "If Brezhnev decided to declare war tomorrow, he would not have hundreds of thousands of Russian prisoners, as Stalin did."

In a different vein, concerning the depoliticization of the Russian people, particularly the youth, the West German Soviet expert Klaus Mehnert noticed that the diminishing interest in Communist ideology has not produced a corresponding surge of interest in anything else except the satisfaction of purely material needs. But isn't it success for Communism to have a completely depoliticized people who are harassed by continual efforts at improving their lamentable material situation? This makes the party's political monopoly more absolute still.

Almost a quarter of a century has passed since Floyd and Mehnert pondered this question. There has been the "liberal" era of Khrushchev, and even if Brezhnev's "neo-Stalinism" is considered, the purges and bloody trials of the 1930s are in the past, and the situation of the average Soviet citizen has improved. In addition, observers agree that no Soviet citizen ever stops complaining and criticizing the regime; nongovernment political publications, in *samizdat,* multiply, and the number of dissidents is increasing at an unexpected rate. But, if you ask any of the dissidents, even one as impetuous as Vladimir Bukovsky, if the regime is threatened, the response is evasive, prudent, sometimes negative. And to the question of whether a liberalization of the regime is possible, the answer is always that this could be accomplished only through an evolutionary process that would take decades.

First double page

1. May Day parade in Moscow. With handsewn red flags, demonstrators converge on Red Square, where they will form a procession.

Second double page

2. Red Square. In the background, the Kremlin. The crowd is due both to the many tourists and to the large GUM department store, on the left, which is the most visited of the capital.

Third double page

3. Two disabled veterans disembark at Sukhumi, in Georgia, Stalin's homeland, where portraits of the "grandfather of all progressive humanity" used to be visible everywhere. Today, it is Lenin who points Soviet citizens toward "Communism, radiant future of all mankind."

4. Every year on May 9, veterans who defeated Hitler's armies reunite in Maxim Gorky Park, in the center of Moscow, to exchange wartime memories.

5. A good-natured veteran is surrounded by the crowd. It isn't his medals that the women, appearing reflective, are looking at: both the smiling man's legs have been amputated.

ЗДРАВСТВУЕТ 1 МАЯ — ДЕНЬ МЕЖДУНА

6. The façade of the Bolshoi Theater is decorated for the First of May with portraits of Marx, Engels, and Lenin. The banner reads "Long live the First of May, day of workers' international solidarity."

Following double page
7. Riga, on the Baltic Sea, has enormous beaches and an invigorating but rarely mild climate. The weather is cool and often cloudy, but the beaches are as crowded as any on the Mediterranean. The visitors here are mostly civil servants or retired. Younger people prefer the Crimea and the warmer seas of the south.

8. At Podolsk, about forty kilometers from Moscow, a retired couple and a village friend enjoy a picnic.

Chapter 2

There Will Be No Russian Bonaparte

The three state "systems" in the USSR — the Party, the KGB, and the army — form a hierarchy that was established in Stalin's time. The team that replaced Stalin in 1953 wasted no time in eliminating his security chief, Beria, the most feared of the troika. Still uneasy about firmly holding the power, Malenkov, Khrushchev, and Bulganin neutralized the security force — then called the NKVD — by purging it as much as possible of Beria's most devoted men. The army helped the Party in this operation, thanks to officers Zhukov and Moskalenko, but did not end up in a position of power. The new Kremlin masters did not intend to allow the army into the privileged position previously occupied by the NKVD. Khrushchev had simply misled these officers, the popular war hero Marshal Zhukov in particular. Once Khrushchev's position was assured, he openly got rid of Zhukov in 1957. Zhukov was not one of the many officers, like Budenny or Timoshenko, who never knew how to respond to Party leaders in any other way than with a "Yes, sir!" Zhukov was the most prominent and high-ranking of the officers. Nonetheless, he headed for retirement in disciplined-soldier fashion, and nothing ever indicated that his discharge caused the slightest rumble; at most there was perhaps a respectful silence.

The subordinate political role the army was to play was evident immediately after the war. The officers who had won the great battles enjoyed immense prestige, and if Stalin had lived longer, a new purge would undoubtedly have been undertaken. In the beginning, he was satisfied with simply downgrading the military and upgrading their enemies and competitors in Beria's police force. Beria was made a marshal; his closest collaborators were promoted to the rank of general. Simultaneously, the commanders who had just distinguished themselves on the front lines disappeared from the public eye, and from the columns of *Pravda*. The cult of the great czarist warlords ended, and the names of Kuznetsov, Suvorov, and Pozharsky were forgotten.

The great demobilization undertaken by Khrushchev in 1960 showed the extent to which the army was bound to the Party. Thousands of officers took early retirement, a measure which, although justified at the end of a war, left many officers with few means of support. Meanwhile, no sign of public discontent was observed; it was Marshal Malinovsky himself who, self-designated, announced this irrevocable decision. It was he who coldly explained that no new position would be given to the greatest military chief, while at the same time Party members like Malenkov and Bulganin had just received posts, however modest. Still, Zhukov was relatively lucky: at his tribunal in October 1957, he was accused of trying to achieve a greater autonomy for the armed forces. Under Stalin, this judgment would have earned him the death sentence. In this case Malinovsky simply said of the hero of Berlin: "I believe that he (Marshal Zhukov) has learned how to fish; he is collecting his pension and writing his memoirs." Khrushchev provided the finishing stroke in a speech at the Military Academy of Moscow, in which he accused Zhukov of violating Leninist principles of leadership in the armed forces and, again, of wanting to separate the army from the Party.

Which brings us to the role of the army as one of the Soviet "apparats." It has always been, and continues to be, a favorite question for amateur historians analyzing Soviet problems. With each change that takes place in the Kremlin, there is a renewed discussion of the possibility of "Bonapartism," or a coup by a military leader, in the Soviet Union. Since Lenin, however, the successive regimes in the USSR, even in times of crisis, have not relied upon the military for direction in the management of political affairs. The case most often cited is that of Nikita Khrushchev, who had summoned a number of army leaders when he had felt his position in the Politburo weaken following de-Stalinization. During the Hungarian uprising of 1956 Khrushchev once more called upon Zhukov, but even in these instances, the army was never anything but an instrument in the hands of the Party. The marshals who were members of the ruling circle — Malinovsky and Voroshilov — shared in the power only as members of the Party apparat, of which they had always been the most submissive servants. They had never acted as the army's representatives.

This legend of a "Soviet Bonapartism" is tied to the sweeping purges in the ranks of the army during the years preceding World War II. There were many people who believed in Stalin's leadership and accepted the official version: thousands of military officers had been involved in plots to overthrow the state. Even the most skeptical found it hard to believe that completely innocent men could be executed, men desperately needed to combat the mounting threat of Nazism. It was thought that there must be at least an element of truth in these accusations, even though the scope of the purge was clearly attributable to Stalin's unreasonable nature. It wasn't yet known that Stalin suffered from a persecution complex, and saw in his leaders *potential* enemies who one day might turn against him. Death or severe punishment was not the result of petty crimes or even criminal intent: men were assassinated whose betrayals existed only in Stalin's wild fantasies. Another proof of this complex came after the war with the execution of the Jewish doctors.

The affair concerning Tukhashevsky, executed in 1937 with eight prominent generals, has contributed to the myth of "Bonapartism." A document was produced that seemed to prove Tukhashevsky's collaboration with the German Secret Service in an attempt to eliminate Stalin. It is known today that the document was a fake, devised by the German and Soviet Secret Services, which then planted it with the Czechoslovak police, who passed it on to Eduard Beneš. Believing it authentic, Beneš promptly gave it to Stalin — who, of course, was aware of it because he had had it made in order to guarantee Tukhashevsky's condemnation at the trial. According to Boris Suvarin, the execution of the "guilty parties" took place without a true trial or deliberation. Stalin drew up, at his pleasure, a list of judges, among whom were prestigious military figures. Ironically, seven of the nine marshals and generals taking part in this "tribunal" were in their turn executed by Stalin. After the Twentieth Party Congress and Khrushchev's secret report, the executed army leaders were rehabilitated with solemnity, and Tukhashevsky was mentioned in the *Komsomolskaya Pravda* as one of the heroes of the USSR.

For years I have been questioning Soviet dissidents about the possibility of a military takeover. Not one will grant that there is any possibility of this; the writer Aleksandr Zinoviev labeled it "completely absurd" in an interview with *Paris Match*. Everyone agrees that the party remains the single instrument capable of exercising power, which it firmly holds with the effective aid of the KBG.

Neither the "Bonapartist" problem nor that of the army's political role would justify further scrutiny here had not an eminent Marxist recently raised the questions, although in a different form. Cornelius Castoriadis, a philosopher and economist who lives in France, wrote in May 1980 on the political role of the army in Soviet society in an essay entitled "Devant la guerre" ["Faced with War"], in his review, *Libre*.

Castoriadis poses a question: how can a country that cannot make a sufficient number of razor blades, eyeglass frames, and other consumer goods, of decent quality; that, after decades of concentrated effort on heavy industry, had to rely on Fiat to build automobile factories and on the West for drilling equipment and products their own satellite countries effortlessly produce — how could such a country then create an armament industry superior to that of the United States'? Castoriadis's answer deserves quoting:

"There is not one Russia; there are two. There is not one Russian 'economy' and one Russian 'national product'; there are two. There is a Russian national product, economy, and life that is 'civilian,' and there is a national product, economy, and life in Russia that is 'military.' 'Civilian' Russia is composed of many sectors. There is the 'official' planning sector (the one that supplies the department stores with inferior goods), and there is a sector reserved for private bureaucratic use (special stores, etc.). The tolerated 'free' sector (the market dealing in certain agricultural products, for example) and the black market sector are also part of 'civilian' Russia. As for the other Russia, it is the result of a systematic skimming of the cream of all the country's resources — first, and most obviously, of human ones — that might be useful to the military section. . . ."

And he continues: "We see two worlds, completely separated — except that the second furnishes the raw material (from coal to foot-soldiers) for the first. It is as if society and economy were perfectly divided into two parts, as if the 'military society' were a distinct group in the 'great Russian society.' 'Growth' (in the capitalist sense of the word) in Russia's economy has been for the most part 'sacrificed' to the army. The skimming process reinforces the effect, for the army takes not simply fifteen engineers out of a hundred; they take the fifteen best." When I read this passage to Vladimir Sichov, he laughed and said, "Your author is wrong. The whole hundred work for the army!" This blunt outburst describes a very real situation which Castoriadis has not ignored: the arms industry is far from being the only one that is part of the army; many areas of production are subordinate to the military. Very large segments of the so-called civilian industry work full-force for the army's needs. In short, Russia is composed of a government, a society, and an economy where absolute and total rank is given to military goals over civilian objectives.

The second point of Castoriadis's "two Russias" theory bears on the question of "Bonapartism." The military class, one can speculate, does not need to exercise political power to conserve or increase its excessive privileges (the equivalent of which can be found only among the elite of the KGB). The history of the Soviet state and, before it, of the czarist empire makes it logical to predict for the foreseeable future the continuation of the Party's political control over the military, even if control entails loading the members of that group with material advantages and prestige. A number of Kremlin-watchers, most

notably Wolfgang Leonhardt, hold this viewpoint. Marxist-educated in the USSR and in East Germany, where he worked in the "propaganda" section for the Ulbricht party before emigrating in 1950 to the German Federal Republic, Leonhardt brings the mark of ten years' personal experience in the USSR to his analyses of Soviet society.

Vladimir Sichov isn't interested in theoretical analysis; his experience of the army is actual and personal. His two years of military duty were spent at the Baykonur space flight center. Because of his engineering degree he was discharged with the rank of second lieutenant. According to Sichov, the army's power is enormous and infinitely greater than that of civilian authority. The effects of this power are felt by everyone, down to the most humble Soviet citizen. If the army needs the best engineers, it will take them. If it deems it necessary to raze an entire neighborhood, or to destroy an eighteenth-century palace because it needs the space, it will be granted the permission to do so. A forest will be felled immediately. The power of the army knows no limits. But, when it comes to exercising government power and determining policy, the military will never be allowed to be involved. A seizure of power by the army is out of the question. No one outside the Politburo can exercise power in the USSR.

As stated earlier, the integral parts of the Soviet government are the Party, the KGB, and the army, the army ranking third. How can the political powers hold the army in a state of allegiance, given its extraordinary strength? It is only through a system established by the Party. In theory, every officer above the rank of major has to become a Party member. As a result, if some high-ranking officer, a general or a marshal, decides to disassociate himself from the official Party line, he will be excluded and forced into retirement. This would eliminate any possibility for a military or political future. There is no more eloquent example of this than the case of Marshal Zhukov, who in the eyes of the army was a god.

Life in a Soviet barracks is both similar to and totally different from that in one elsewhere in Europe. Shared living quarters, hazing of recruits, and mediocre food are part of army life everywhere. But, while the Soviet people outside the larger cities are badly nourished, those in the army are fed three meals a day. Thirty years ago, shortages were such that army life was preferable to civilian life. Aleksandr Zinoviev, born in the countryside, reported that it wasn't until he slept in barracks that he saw bedsheets. The lowest-class recruit receives a monthly sum of 3.50 rubles, about $5.47, enough to buy about ten packs of cigarettes at about 30 or 35 kopecks a package. The pay increases for a noncommissioned officer, but does not exceed 15 rubles a month ($23.44). If an N.C.O. decides to stay in the army, he has a chance of earning up to 100 rubles a month ($156.25). Sichov received such a salary because of his education. Toward the end of his service, he was making 200 rubles ($305), which would be considered a very good civilian salary. Those with a college education are encouraged to stay in the army, and offered advantages and the chance for promotion because the army lacks officers.

But the daily life and living conditions of the Soviet soldier still appear to be more strenuous than those of Western soldiers. The Soviet soldier rises at 6:30 A.M. for thirty minutes of calisthenics; he then must straighten his bunk and clean his boots. After an 8 o'clock breakfast, he goes to his assigned station. There is no break, except for noontime lunch. The officers arrive at 9 A.M. and leave the barracks at 6 P.M., but the soldiers, even at that hour, are not free: every afternoon there are "political instruction" courses. Their only "personal time" is between 9 and 10 P.M. For a Soviet soldier there is no normal leave either: leave is considered a reward for good conduct. If granted, a furlough could be two weeks, but one could also go two years without one day of leave.

There are other things that can cause a sensible man to turn away from army service: the absurdity of certain established protocols, for example. When a high-ranking military leader such as a marshal visits a unit, its commanding officers enter into a state of excitement bordering on hysteria. Sichov saw, in his own unit, grass being dyed greener, and even snow being dyed! "Snow? But what color?" "White; it was dirty, you see." He also heard that in another unit the soldiers polished the sidewalk leading to the entrance of a barracks, with brushes, on the night preceding the arrival of a group of marshals.

Of prime concern in the army is the question of combat readiness. "Iron discipline reigns in the army," Sichov reflects, "and high-level political instruction is mandatory. Moreover, the Soviet soldier knows more than most that one never questions an order. What the *zampolit*, the equivalent of the 'political commissar' of the last war, tells them is absolute, Biblical truth, an order, and also a rule for conduct. The *zampolit* [the word is the abbreviation for 'political assistant to the commander'] is in charge of ideology; curiously, all of the soldiers have complete confidence in what he tells them. For example, during the Afghanistan affair, they were told that the army was there because there was an exterior danger to the USSR, and everyone believed that. During the Prague crisis of 1968 the *zampolits* had explained to their soldiers that the German Federal Republic was going to invade Czechoslovakia and that the Soviet army was to be there first. The soldiers believed that too. When I told them, 'But look, if the Germans had invaded Czechoslovakia, that would have been World War Three,' it didn't change their 'truth,' for it was the 'truth' of the political commissar. Today, morale is very high, and discipline is faultless. This is the great difference from the Americans who, in Vietnam, went to spend their weekends in Saigon. We know the results. Such a thing is completely out of the question for the Soviet military, whether they are soldiers or officers: there would be a court-martial and they would be mercilessly shot."

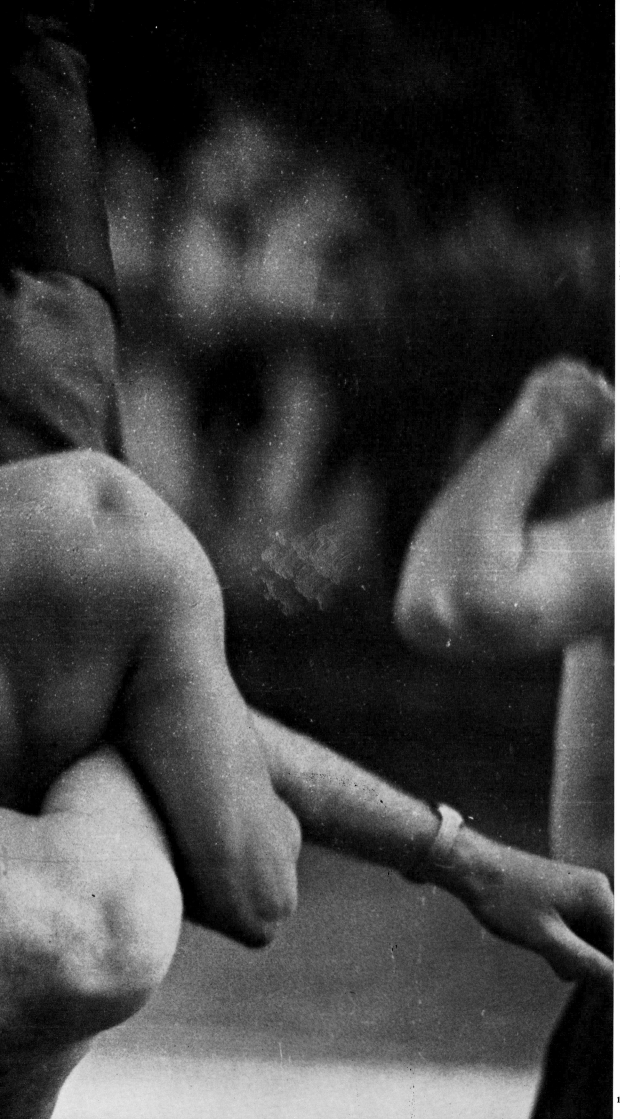

First double page
9.   The typical day of the
Soviet recruit begins at six
o'clock with thirty minutes
of running and calisthenics.
Discipline here is much
more strict than in any
other European army. In
addition, recruits attend
interminable political
indoctrination meetings.

10.   After their intensive
training, the soldiers from
the "domestic units"
(charged with protecting
Party officials and other
important persons) are
superior athletes.

11. Vladimir Sichov served in the army at the Baykonur Cosmodrome, a launching site for the Soviet manned space flights. On his epaulet, his first second-lieutenant star. On the left is a young soldier, on the right an officer from his company.

12. These young men, most of them students, are about to board railroad cars that will carry them to a harsh two years of military service. While waiting, they console each other by singing to a guitar accompaniment.

13. For the Russian, boots have always been objects of solicitous care.

Previous double page
14. The training of certain special "shock troop" units resembles that of the Marines. Future commandos work out in close combat. These units are destined for the Kremlin security guard; they ensure the safety of the ministries and the buildings where international meetings take place.

15. This recruit from a southern province tightly hugs his machine gun, a particularly prized weapon.

16. Whatever the season, the daily calisthenics session takes place outdoors.

17. The authorities show a predilection for gymnastics requiring strength.

18, 19, 20. The recruits get to know the barracks grounds by sweeping the courtyard. No broom: bundles of branches must suffice. Only the day before, they were still students at Kazan, where Lenin studied law.

Following double page
21. The specialized troops at the Baykonur Cosmodrome. In winter uniforms and heavy gray-green coats, with their cap earflaps up and their boots carefully waxed, these elite soldiers pass in review before officers who monitor their impeccable dress.

Chapter 3

The Soviet Woman

During the early stages of the Revolution, Lenin wrote that managing the politics and affairs of the socialist state would be so simple that any housewife could assume the task. No managing housewife, however, has made an appearance throughout the history of the Bolshevik Party. The only exception in whom the Soviets can take pride was also one of the first female diplomats in history. No one would recognize Lenin's "housewife" in Mme. Aleksandra Kollontai, aristocrat turned Social Democrat. Even more advanced than other feminists of her day, she appears to have been in the vanguard of women's liberation. Not satisfied simply with the suffragette struggle for voting equality, in the early 1920s she also advocated sexual and moral liberation, both inconceivable at the time. Kollontai, an impetuous militant, also led the struggle for true workers' unions; she underwrote the famous "worker opposition" group inside the Party, and was even elected to the Central Committee. She quickly disagreed with the general policy and was forced out. She was sent as ambassador to Norway, then to Stockholm, and then to Mexico, where she spent a total of fifteen years until 1945.

Inez Armand, who won Lenin's boundless affection with her intelligence and beauty, also preached sexual liberty, with the help of shock treatments if necessary, as well as street demonstrations of nude women. She believed that the sexual act should become as simple as eating. Her ideas shocked Lenin, but did not hinder their extensive correspondence about women, family, and love.

Sexuality was never mentioned, for Vladimir Ilitch was a radical puritan, conforming to the period's revolutionary rigor. All of this, however, belongs to the glorious past of the first post-Revolutionary years. Very quickly women's liberation became the least of the Bolsheviks' worries. In terms of her character, the Soviet woman of today is thought by some to be stronger than the Soviet man. Any contact with the wives of dissidents or political prisoners is striking: One is confronted with extremely energetic, unshakable women. They have challenged the police, made the rounds of KGB headquarters, even spoken with camp officials in order to get what they wanted, whether it is an extra visit, or a letter or package delivered. They have stimulated international campaigns on their husbands' behalf with stubborn zeal. The role of these wives — whose physiques often correspond to the force of their character — has been decisive in their husbands' release. Names cannot be mentioned, of course, but a significant number of examples attest to this. Some are quite graphic: one woman was in the midst of a very unhappy, often abusive marriage, which finally ended in divorce. The woman remarried a very prosperous man, quit her own job, and enjoyed a life of relative luxury by Soviet standards. However, when her ex-husband was arrested and sent to a camp, she divorced her new husband and dropped everything in order to work for his release. Daily she went to the KGB, and in the end managed to get permission to remarry her ex-husband, in his Siberian camp, so that she could be more effective in obtaining his freedom. For the same reason, she also got a court to reinstate him as the father of her children — he had been stripped of paternity rights as a political prisoner. All this is perhaps not so striking to a Westerner, but the simple fact of marrying a prisoner, and especially of reestablishing his paternal authority, is a gigantic feat in the USSR. When she finally obtained his freedom, she divorced him again four days later.

In the new world he was feverishly constructing, Lenin did not forget women. He promised them complete legal emancipation and equality, and believed in the consequent equal division of labor. Literally applied, this meant that women would occupy the same positions as men and would be compelled to perform difficult tasks. With equal rights come equal duties. In his time, the concept seemed justified, but it has been perpetuated into our day. Even Soviet propaganda publishes pictures of women working in factory construction or as members of shock troops whose exploits have been celebrated in the literature of socialist realism. In Sichov's photographs, women can be seen working in train stations, sweeping snowy streets at $-30°$, and pouring asphalt under the hot sun.

Women make up the majority of the population (56 percent) and of the work force (52 percent). Today, it is inconceivable that a woman in the Soviet Union, especially an unmarried woman, should remain unemployed: she would find herself in an uncomfortable, suspicious position. Only wives of Academy members, generals, or other representatives of the new upper class may not work. Child care, study, and meal preparation are a thousand times harder for the Soviet woman, because preschools and day-care centers are crowded and costly. The fee is between 10 and 15 percent of a monthly salary, about $18.70 to almost $29. Waiting lines are never-ending for the slightest purchase; electric appliances are scarce and of inferior quality. One solution to the problem is the famour *babushka,* the Russian grandmother who lives with the family and cares for the children, but not every household has a grandmother. There is an alarming decrease in the birthrate in the European USSR, which stems in large part from the sheer difficulty of raising a family of several children, despite the regime's efforts to encourage larger families through family aid and paid pregnancy leaves. Those overwhelming difficulties account for the growing number of abortions — the most widely used method of birth control. Abortions, freely allowed, are inexpensive even by Soviet standards:

5 rubles, or $7.80. The pill is less popular in the Soviet Union than in the West, and does not seem to have been perfected, as is also true for the IUD.

Dr. Mikhail Stern, in his book *Sex in the USSR,* makes a strong statement about sexual life in the Soviet Union. His broad clinical experience has led him to conclude that the Soviet man has more sexual problems than his Western counterpart. The consequences are that women are more and more detached from their mates in both day-to-day attitudes and romantic matters. A mediocre and frequently alcoholic lover — most often, he is completely drunk during sexual encounters — the Soviet male can appear to his wife or mistress not only as cowed in front of the authorities, but constantly making concessions to the regime's demands in order to conserve his meager salary. Soviet women thus live more and more among themselves. Love is often replaced by a somewhat maternal feeling of pity: "I feel sorry for him," they say to their friends, more often than "I love him." Husband and wife usually take separate vacations; the wife will often go with a friend, although lesbianism is infrequent. It exists, chiefly among the intelligentsia, and is not forbidden by law, simply because the phenomenon was extremely rare before the Revolution, as in other Slavic countries. Homosexuality in men, on the other hand, is punishable by up to six years in a camp. Unmarried couples cohabiting are freely accepted by all, as are children born out of wedlock, and the Soviet woman's mixed feelings about her husband or lover does not stop her from having her child. Often she will simply choose not to live with the father. The evolution of the Soviet woman's condition can be perceived in two ways: as a necessary consequence of the USSR's conditions of life, or as a sign of convergence between socialist and capitalist systems.

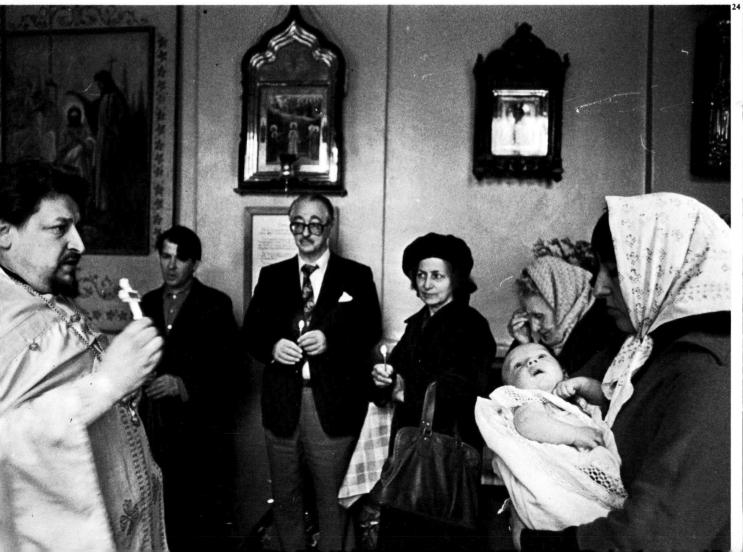

Previous double page
22. Aïda, Vladimir Sichov's wife, in their communal apartment in Moscow. Marshal Ney lived in this house, one of the few that escaped the Moscow fire. There is neither hot water nor a bathroom. To give her son, Nikita, a bath, Aïda had to heat water in the kitchen, then fill a plastic tub.

23. Aïda in front of the house in the Crimea where the family lived for a while.

24. Baptisms are celebrated three times a week in Orthodox churches. Here, peasants have come to attend a ceremony. In the large churches, several newborn babies are baptized at a time.

25. A "communal" kitchen in Moscow. This term has no ideological significance; a communal lodging is simply one shared by two or more families. Rent is very low in the USSR, but all the tenants must use the single kitchen and bathroom in the apartment. In Leningrad, the situation is worse: often in some of the larger houses five to ten families live together. In Sichov's case, there were only two, these two gas stoves show.

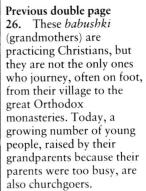

30. Since the Revolution, Soviet women have worked alongside the men, in the most strenuous jobs. But being a waitress, especially in the buffet-style cafés, is considered both privileged and lucrative.

31. In Vologda, women do their washing in the river, as they have for centuries.

31

32. Women laborers spread asphalt on a street in Kazan.

33. In Moscow, women rake autumn leaves with primitive brooms made from dried branches.

34. A furrier in Kazan works on skins under Spartan conditions, with few accommodations for personal comfort or hygiene.

Chapter 4

Russia Lives Less Well Than the Other Republics

As in every domain, the Bolshevik Party's policy regarding the ethnic nationalities within the Russian Empire rapidly evolved immediately following the Revolution. In 1915, Lenin had written, "Russia is a prison of peoples . . . ; the Russian proletariat cannot fight for socialist revolution without recognizing their own unrestrained freedom to secede from Russia. This is true for all nations oppressed by czarism."

The following year, he estimated that at least 57 percent of the population suffered from this sort of oppression, and repeated, ". . . It follows that recognition of the right to secede [for these nations] is essential." He continued to proclaim this principle over the next two or three years. It was written into the first Soviet constitution and is valid for the present one.

The regime's liberal attitude toward minority nations living on Russian territory did not spring solely from an abstract commitment to the causes of peoples struggling for their freedom. Lenin counted on the element of nationalism to ensure the success of the Revolution. The non-Russian peoples would rise up against their czarist oppressor and then embrace with enthusiasm the new Soviet Union, which assured them autonomy within a federal framework. Lenin very quickly abandoned these generous principles, and the Bolshevik regime's centralized authority in Moscow encompassed the outlying republics. The constitutional right to secede became a theoretical formula, and was put to the test only once: an Armenian group decided to petition for an autonomous Armenian Soviet Socialist Republic. The immediate result: the group was dissolved and the leaders sent to Siberia. Certain ethnic groups whose sole demand concerned respect for their traditions have been sent *en masse* to gulag camps.

The system set up by the Bolsheviks has very often been considered an imperialist one, in that it perpetuated under a new flag czarist oppression of minority peoples. Simultaneously, exterior expansion has been pursued under the guise of an international workers' movement. The czarist state was often seen as a classic colonial empire, unusual only in that, instead of being separated from the motherland by an ocean or sea, its colonized peoples were simply across its frontiers. That had no effect on the subordinate role they played in the empire's decision making in Moscow.

Today, the Russian government conserves its centralizing and imperialist nature but, according to a number of dissidents who have come from the Soviet Union, the Russian people, the greatest in number and those whose capital remains the seat of power, live in worse conditions than the people of any other republic in the Soviet Union. This is certainly true in the case of peoples who have a markedly lower cultural and political development: for instance, in the southern Moslem republics, where the population benefits not only from better economic conditions but also from greater liberty. This fact, however, does not at all hinder the local bureaucrats from maintaining a feudal system of exorbitant privileges.

In the southern areas, the Russians, especially bureaucrats from Moscow, are held in very low esteem. In Azerbaijan and Kazakhstan, engineers and other specialists who have come from the capital are treated with scornful condescension by the inhabitants. Because of this frosty reception, many Russians will refuse jobs in these areas. Aleksandr Zinoviev says bluntly: "In the USSR, it is not the center of the empire that exploits the colonial peoples; it is those peoples who exploit the center."

The Soviet regime has not failed simply in its efforts to create a new mankind. It must have also realized that the Revolution and the subsequent government have not fundamentally modified the various nations that are subordinate to it. What has remained intact, and even become stronger because of Moscow's political pressure, is the nationalism in the Moslem republics. One cannot assume, however, that an Iranian parallel can be easily drawn here — the religious factor is not the primary one. In fact, specifically national qualities (both good and bad) of these peoples seem reinforced. One of the most important traits seems to be a passive resistance directed toward the Soviet system, administered by the local Party structures. This system is often seen (and rightly so) as a foreign power. In practice, the form that this resistance most often takes is corruption: a highly lucrative activity for those local officials who take part. The leaders of the local Parties buy Moscow's goodwill with gifts, their value equivalent to the rank of the central official. At home, they get back this "invested capital" through widespread bribes, which extend up and down the state bureaucratic ladder. We have a document to graphically illustrate this for us: Ilya Zemtzov, a senior official, has written a book that reveals the observations of a long administrative career in Azerbaijan.

Bribery and baksheesh are not limited to the Asian republics. In the Soviet Union as a whole, as in most of its satellite countries, it is now a permanent aspect of the economic system. Salaries are not only low, they are insufficient to assure means of livelihood, even for a population that is accustomed to near-starvation living standards. Supplementary income is necessary, but in an economic system of severely controlled collectivism, it is illegal. To earn more by doing more than the required work on a job is possible only in theory. In the first place, the requirements are already very high, and the necessary extra effort doesn't seem worth it. Second, and most important, when the norms or quotas are surpassed, the regime revises the norm upward to conform with that extra work.

Illegal labor, however, present everywhere in the USSR, is most widespread in the Moslem republics of the south. It automatically engenders generalized corruption, because, in order for it to work, official "complacency" must be bought. In Moscow and in the larger industrial regions, the officials in charge have simply chosen to close their eyes to these practices, as long as they are performed quietly and discreetly. They do so in order for the system to continue functioning; they also do it out of an understanding of the workers' plight, since even at their own level, they live in a constant atmosphere of want. They know that the workers cannot get by on their salaries. There is a saying that is common everywhere in the Soviet sphere, and sums up the situation: "They ['they' is a plural that, in the Soviet bloc, always designates Communists] lie to us when pretending to pay us; we lie to them when pretending to work."

In the outlying republics that have a tradition of near-feudal employee-employer relationships, the employer's docility is bought through bribery. Once the offer is accepted, a parallel economic system of true "under-ground" production develops. It functions as well as possible on every level. It begins with smaller farmers who produce more melons or tomatoes than required of their *kolkhoz*. They sell the produce while ignoring the required norms that they must deliver to the state markets. This cheating rises through the whole structure, and ends with the highest officials.

Sometimes, corruption gets so out of hand that Moscow is forced to respond. One of the most striking examples is that of Aliyev, himself of Moslem decent, whom the Party put in charge of cleaning up the Augean stables of Azerbaijan. The means he came up with were clever. Control of Azerbaijani policy was to be handed over to representatives of that elite corps, carefully trained, privileged, and therefore loyal to the Soviet regime: the KGB! Unfortunately, we cannot elaborate each chapter of this tale: sent to combat corruption, the agents from Moscow ended up being corrupted by the system, which was too widespread and too firmly established.

No region or area of the Soviet Union escapes this endemic corruption. Our choice of the Moslem republics merely illustrates the diversity of the regions under the centralized force of Moscow. Sichov, camera in hand, traveled through these provinces. His photographs illustrate the contrasts that make Soviet reality so difficult to understand. These contrasts are more obvious in the republics than they are in European Russia. Here, the newest class is not composed only of *apparatchky* or other privileged persons of the regime; it is made up of a picturesque fauna of enriched profiteers, resembling even in their dress flashy millionaire adventurers out of the Latin American thirties. At the same time, a miserable downtrodden and starving group make up the Oriental proletariat, still denied — and spared — socialist indoctrination. Their poverty is perhaps greater than that of the European regions of the Soviet Union, but at least the regime lets them live in peace to pursue their own ancestral traditions and customs, without obliging them to follow its policies. Here again, the Soviet system perpetuates the colonialist attitude it inherited from the czarist empire.

Previous double pages

35. In the Kazakh Republic these primitive desert dwellings are located less than 2 kilometers away from Baykonur Cosmodrome's launching pads.

36. Men still spend many hours in cafés in Samarkand in Uzbek, as in the rest of the Orient, despite the slogans glorifying the October Revolution that cover the wall. Above are portraits of members of the Politburo.

37. It is the hour of prayer in Samarkand for these men, who have maintained their Moslem faith.

38. These children in Kazakh, with their distinctly Asiatic features and a centuries-old culture, live only one half mile from the Baykonur Cosmodrome.

Chapter 5

Young People Are More Interested in Pop Music Than in Ideology

Although Russian youth have been the center of painstaking political care and attention since the first post-Revolutionary years, a widespread political apathy now characterizes the Soviet young. Their rejection of politics results from the regime's determination to impose one party line or doctrine, outside which no divergent political action or thought is permitted. In this as in other matters, the regime's successive and various attempts have produced contradictory results.

Immediately after the October Revolution, the Party's objectives were clearly defined: destroy the old order down to its very foundation, "in the cities and the countryside," and begin constructing a new socialist society. These goals were truly revolutionary in their aim to mobilize not only the mass of workers, but also the youth and the intellectuals: scientists, writers, and artists. In the first difficult and challenging years of the young Bolshevik state, arts and letters soared in a way they have not since.

It took only a few years for Bolshevism to break any revolutionary spirit: the rule of the Party and its rigid bureaucracy were quickly established. Concerning the young, the regime's first and foremost concern was to raise them in the Communist faith. Toward this end, the Komsomol (the Young Communist League) was created. Like the other mass organizations, the Komsomol was an arm of the Party established to promote political ideas. This goal served merely to alienate its young members, not just because a political choice was denied them, but also because even simple discussions were "organized," never spontaneous. Whatever the topic, announced in advance, its conclusions were foregone: *Pravda* had already determined them in its editorial broadcast that same morning before the Soviet people left for work.

It took a dozen years of this political preprogramming to bring about, first, a progressive decline of interest in political topics, and then the thorough depoliticization of the young. They turned away from politics because they felt powerless to influence events. In Stalin's time, it was clear that no individual action could change anything. During the years of relative liberalization — Malenkov's ephemeral reign, then the Khrushchev era, for example — everyone knew that any view expressed would have to be in line with the Party's. A saying from the czarist period, "Leaders know better," expresses this passive attitude the Soviets have toward authority.

Klaus Mehnert, considered an expert on the Soviet Union, born in Russia and widely traveled, has noted that since the middle of the 1950s a secondary consequence of this depoliticization has taken place, a change in the academic disciplines chosen for study. The young are turning toward the more technical fields and abandoning the humanities. There are no university departments of political science in the USSR. Instead, another class, the bane of a young Communist's existence, replaces these courses during the intermediate high school years: *diamat*. Hiding under this abbreviation is dialectical materialism, the backbone of all branches of study. Whether you are becoming a doctor, a veterinarian or surgeon, a concert pianist or agronomist, you have absolutely no chance of succeeding without passing the *diamat* exams, and one other subject of universal import: the abridged course on the history of the Communist Party of the Soviet Union. In the eastern republics, this last course also includes the history of each individual national Communist Party. But the true nightmare continues to be *diamat*. One of the cornerstones of Marxist doctrine, dialectical materialism is not one of the simplest of the prophet's teachings. No amount of "popularizing" can make it more digestible for the young, who, in the large part, come from the country. In addition, they question the usefulness of these enigmatic formulas that they must commit to memory for recitation without real understanding of their meaning.

Creating unswerving Communists for the future was the Komsomol's task. Twenty years ago, it had 18,000,000 to 19,000,000 members. On January 1, 1979, there were 39,000,000 among its ranks. Today the Komsomol's goals are only remotely related to its original plans. Work brigades are formed to help peasants harvest; hours of toil are donated to prepare for state holidays. Campaigns are organized to channel youthful enthusiasm toward projects considered of vital nationwide importance, like the virgin land clearing announced by Khrushchev. The projects that fall to the Komsomol are not always that innocent, however. When the young start formulating opinions out of line with the regime's, they can be distracted from them by campaigns organized to occupy their free time. This was notably true during the Hungarian uprising in 1956: at the beginning of the following year countless work brigades left Russia to help build the new regime, which was lacking in strong arms.

Obviously this depoliticization can be considered a setback for the regime in its attempt to create enthusiasm for the future of Communism. One can speculate that even a small amount of freedom in Komsomol discussions would have stimulated political feeling, and though there would obviously be those who disagreed with general Party line, confrontation would no doubt have encouraged young fervent Communists to defend Party policies. Instead, after the enthusiasm of the first years, Komsomol meetings have been overtaken by apathy: *grayness* is the word the official Soviet press itself has used.

But the Komsomol plays another important role for the Party: it is the breeding ground for young "managers" for its bureaucracy. Several important leaders have come from the Komsomol. Oftentimes, the "young" have remained in the league well after their fortieth year. Aleksandr Chelepin, former First Secretary, is one example. He had an active role in the KGB and was called "Iron Churik" — "Churik" is the diminutive of "Aleksandr." (Felix Dzerzhinsky, who as head of the Cheka, the original security police force, organized the first bloody purges after the Revolution, was called "Iron Felix.") Semilchasni is another example. After Pasternak had been awarded the Nobel Prize, Semilchasni stated in public that this beloved Russian poet was worse than a pig, because at least a pig does not soil his eating place. Deservedly, V. Semilchasni was named vice president of the Ukrainian Council of Ministers.

It is never easy to analyze Soviet life. To say that the Soviet youth are *depoliticized* is true but inexact. Perhaps it is better to say that the word has slightly different meanings depending on whether it is used in the USSR or in the West. Because the only arena for political action is within official Communism, they have become completely uninterested. They are not, however, politically insensitive. On the contrary, they hunger to *know;* they listen to foreign radio broadcasts and devour any book

that is not an official tract. They debate current issues endlessly at the universities, in their dorm rooms, or in public parks, in the best tradition of the Russian intelligentsia. They manage, through great effort, to keep abreast of political life outside the Soviet Union, familiarizing themselves with the names of contemporary philosophers and sometimes even their works, though access to these is restricted to the regime's academicians and researchers. There are also those who have Soviet degrees in the field of English, although, in the USSR, British literature stops with Byron and Charles Dickens, and Hemingway is considered avant-garde. Zinoviev maintains that people read much more in the USSR than in the West. That is literally true, but it is also true that the choice of foreign authors available is severely limited. "Progressive" writers from Turkey or Outer Mongolia, from Korea or Vietnam, are touted as authors of immortal masterpieces.

The young Soviet's attitude toward the West is based on the most fragmentary information, and is very hard to analyze. We tend to judge them badly, and they are severely criticized by the regime. It is believed that they know only the least important things about the West: its clothing styles, blue jeans, T-shirts, rock, disco, and (probably by now) reggae, but then again, this type of knowledge is the easiest to obtain. Records are brought in from the West, and as the latest hits are taped, cassettes multiply at amazing speed. Interest in America has reached "fad" proportions. But while the young know the history of jazz or the names of American rock groups better than their Western elders, they remain unaware of the existence of the Bill of Rights, or the procedures of presidential election.

It seems today, after a half-century of bureaucratic Communist reign, that maybe this youthful apathy will turn out to be exactly what the regime intended: a youth insensitive to political problems, whose ability to judge has been reduced to simple formulas and slogans, and who have lost interest in asking questions or reflecting.

Previous double pages

39. Private schools, though tolerated, are not permitted under Soviet law and could be closed at any time. Older professors teach children of the more wealthy families music, dance, and even skating.

40. Often schoolchildren are organized into "work brigades." They render free services like the street cleaning shown here, in order to learn to appreciate the value of physical labor.

41. Gorky Street in the center of Moscow. The older generation is bemused by the fashions of the young, who are attracted, in the USSR as elsewhere, to exotic clothing.

42. In Tuapse, citizens join in celebrating the First of May. These budding color-guards are "*Oktobriaky*," Children of the October Revolution, the organization youngsters join when they reach school age.

43, 44. These scenes in Leningrad and Kazan would have been unthinkable during the period of revolutionary puritanism, when public displays of affection would have been reported.

45. The marriage ceremony, even civil, still holds its attraction, despite the Bolsheviks' attempt to reduce it to a simple matter of registration. An official at the registry presents the marriage certificate to a young couple, who have waited three months since making their marriage request.

46. The ritual kiss and traditional bouquet of gladioli do not guarantee a long-lasting union: in Moscow, one marriage out of two ends in divorce.

47. There are several marriage bureaus in Moscow. For formal ceremonies, couples prefer the luxurious office in downtown Moscow on Griboyedov Street, where Christina Onassis was married. The young still try for a touch of ceremony on special occasions: the dark suit is obligatory, the Young Communists wear neckties, and girls dream of the traditional white gown.

Following double page
48. The pop music group Stas-Namin has millions of fans throughout the country. The group was started by former Soviet President Anastas Mikoyan's grandson, who has the same first name, thus the nickname "Stas," which is part of the group's name.

Chapter 6

Dissidents Can Be Traditionalist or Democratic

What is a dissident? First of all, a dictionary will help us little. Whatever the authority, one standard definition is given: *dissident* connotes a stance in disagreement with a particular doctrine subscribed to by the majority, or by an official church. It might seem at first that this meaning could easily be applied to the Soviet- or Eastern-bloc dissidents. They reject the term, however. In the *gulag,* or confronted with *sbirri* from the KGB, a defenseless man does not quibble over nuances of meaning. To deny being a dissident is, first of all, a defense. It is like saying, in effect, to the executioner or KGB official, "We are not attacking the system at all. We do not want to change it. Besides, how could we? We just do not agree." Do not agree with what? With nothing in particular. Simply do not agree. The dissidents have found another word to refer to themselves, this time, in Russian. They declare themselves *inakomisliashchiye,* those "thinking differently."

This neologism is difficult to translate, and is used only in the USSR. Generally, under a totalitarian regime, "thinking differently" simply means to think at all. Under Hitler, it was said, "The Führer thinks for us." In the USSR, those in power do not ask others to think as they do; they hardly think at all, but instead simply give orders and provide slogans. By declaring themselves not as resisting, but as "thinking differently," dissidents score a double victory. At the same time, they demonstrate that thinking freely is denied them, and they also take refuge in a faultless system of defense: we have done nothing and intend to do nothing. We merely "think differently."

For simplicity, I will use the term *dissident* and begin with those who have managed to come to the West. To those who try arbitrarily to group dissidents together, one thing is particularly striking: they are actually very divided among themselves, sometimes by insuperable differences. To be lumped together annoys them as much as it amuses their Communist enemies. Since they have suffered under the same regime and endured the same hardships, it is easy for us to suggest that they should team up in support of a common cause. But the divisions between them in the Soviet Union are all the more striking once they are in the West, and this is only right. First, it is fortunate that their new-found freedom of thought and expression is resulting in fresh discussion and even dispute. Also, they have lived under a monolithic regime

all their lives, where no political pluralism was permitted. Those who have come to the West are the most active, the most politicized, and the most militant. To give in again, this time to a different monolith, would certainly signal a poor end to a long struggle.

The differences of opinion dissidents carry with them into exile are the very same ones that divided them in their own country. The opposition movements in the USSR are composed of several varied groups, but there is general agreement, based on what certain participants have said, that the true political dissidents fall into three broad categories.

THE NEO-MARXISTS

In the USSR, everyone is subjected to Marxist-Leninist indoctrination. Young people have all gone through Party organizations — the *Oktobriaky,* the Pioneers, and finally, the Komsomol — until the end of their secondary or university schooling. It is not enough to say simply that they have had Marxist-Leninist training. They have had that and only that from a very early age. It would be a miracle if generations raised under these conditions should not harbor the conviction, acquired in adolescence, that Marxism-Leninism represents the whole truth, the best total explanation of the world.

The typical neo-Marxist of today has not rid himself of this background. But he has added another, more realistic, reason to explain his persistence in defending the Marxist-Leninist teachings of his youth: this regime has lasted more than half a century and has destroyed all traces of the past. While they are in the USSR, dissidents of this type claim to follow a very pure Marxism, free of Stalinist taint. Dissidents as violent and inflexible as General Grigorenko began by rallying under this neo-Marxist banner and did not, even faced with their executioners, stop preaching their faith in the pure doctrine.

Roy Medvedev's case is particularly interesting. A great historian whose works on the Revolution and the Stalin era have been published only in the West, he still lives freely in Moscow but is deprived of the right to work at his profession. From time to time he makes statements that could bring him before the KGB. He is tolerated partly because he is well known, but mostly because he continues to call himself an orthodox Marxist. During the last elections for the Supreme Soviet, a purely pro forma ceremony as are all Soviet elections, he tried something unusual. Invoking a point of law — staying within the legal framework, whenever possible, is an unfailing concern for all dissidents — he presented "free" candidates, ones who did not belong to the Communist Party. This completely unrealistic gesture was unprecedented in the USSR.

THE DEMOCRATIC MOVEMENT

In *Will the Soviet Union Survive until 1984?*, published in 1970, the dissident historian Andrei Amalrik characterized what he called the "cultural opposition" in the USSR this way: it is a mass movement with countless sympathizers, who express their discontent only "in the bedroom," as the Russian expression goes. They base their liberal ideology on a belief in a Western type of society, on a parliamentary democracy — adapted, however, to the specific conditions of Russian life.

Sakharov's group would be in this category. He published one of the first true programs for a democratic government in the USSR; it was immediately picked up by the international press.

On November 4, 1970, Sakharov founded the "Committee for Human Rights," and he has ceaselessly addressed in his own and in its name declarations to the free world announcing the more flagrant abuses and violations of these rights by the Soviet regime. The founders of the group, all eminent physicists, wanted to form a nonpolitical association to defend human rights on the basis of national and international laws, and even clauses in the Soviet Constitution itself. The three founding members, Andrei Sakharov, Andrei Tverdokhlebev, and Valery Chalidze, were joined by Aleksandr Volpin, a poet and a mathematician who is the son of the famous revolutionary poet Sergei Esenin, who committed suicide in 1925, and by Boris Zuckermann, a physics professor. Six months after its founding, the committee became affiliated with the Human Rights League and maintained close contact with it until Sakharov's expulsion.

THE RUSSIAN TRADITIONALISTS

From the very beginning of the nineteenth century, two groups clashed while struggling for a liberalization of the autocratic czarist regime. The first group, called *Zapadniki* (from the Russian word for West), envisioned a democracy whose institutions would be borrowed from the West. The Slavophiles were opposed to this vision. They favored a return to the wellsprings of Russian national tradition (*Vietchnya Russ*) and to the Orthodox Church.

Taking into account many differences arising from the passage of time, the Slavophiles call to mind a third group of dissidents, inspired by an ideology that could be defined as Christian. Its undisputed head is Aleksandr Solzhenitsyn, who by virtue of his personality, his literary genius, and his courage also dominates the other dissident groups, despite the divisions among them. Even those who totally oppose his ideas on the grounds that they are outmoded or no longer valid publicly acknowledge that not only has he made the world aware of the Soviet prison camp — recall that just a dozen years ago the number of those who understood the meaning of the word *gulag* could be counted on one hand — but also that he has accomplished a task that was previously thought impossible: he has turned the European Communist intelligentsia away from a blind submission to Moscow. This is the movement to which the most prominent dissidents belong: the Bukovskys, Maximovs, Ginzburgs, and Gorbanevskayas.

Like those of the democratic movement, the traditionalists do not see themselves as a political group; they stress ethical values. Their foundation is essentially Christian-Orthodox. Its representatives believe, justly, that Communism has destroyed the national, cultural, and social fabric of the nation, and has smothered its traditional values.

These major opposition groups are all represented by an intellectual and "cultural" elite, in Amalrik's words. The spokesmen for these groups are mostly exiles, banished by the regime, but there are also countless numbers of small opposition cells inside the country championing the rights of minorities, various religious groups, workers, peasants, etcetera. Their members people the *gulags*, even though their names are not known outside the country. We would be aggravating this injustice if we were not to mention them here, however briefly.

49. Painter Yuri Gerasimov, shown dancing on a chair to the sound of an ancient record player, belonged to the avant-garde movement at its start in the 1950s. Today, he is officially recognized and his canvases are displayed in state exhibits. It is not a joyous occasion he celebrates: this photograph was taken on the day he was forced out of his old but spacious and picturesque house. The authorities had decided to raze it and give him a two-room apartment instead.

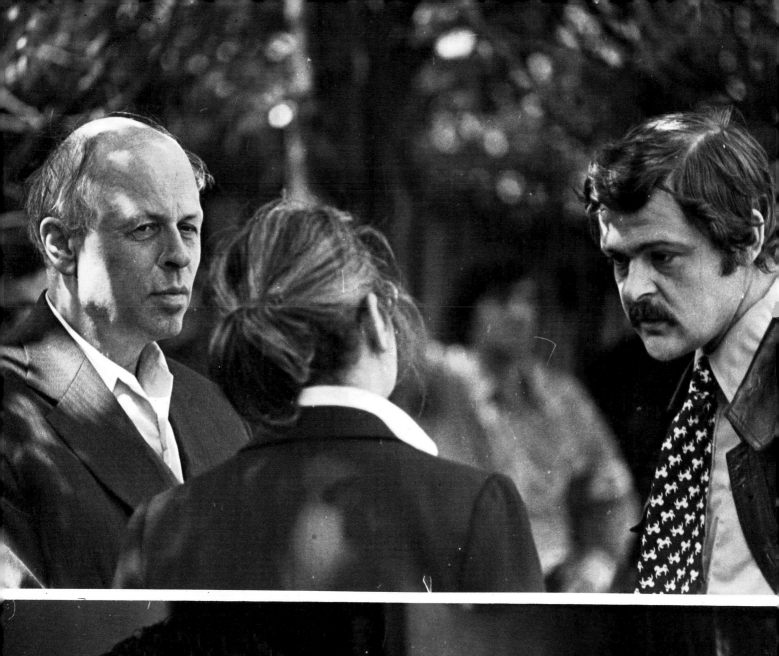

Previous double page
50. This photograph was taken at the Sichov residence during a gathering in honor of an exhibit of the works of painter Mikhail Chemiakin. Chemiakin later moved to Paris when his paintings were deemed too "modernist" and censored by the regime. A number of well-known intellectuals came to see them at the Sichovs': from right to left, Georgi Vladimov, author of *Faithful Rustan*, Aleksandr Zinoviev, Venedikt Erofeyev, author of *Moscow to the End of the Line*, the geologist poet Vyacheslav Lion, and their wives. On the extreme left, Aïda Sichov.

51. Andrei Sakharov, the nuclear physicist, is the acknowledged spokesman for the Soviet dissidents and the founder of the Moscow Human Rights League. His prestige is enormous, his name familiar to every Russian. He was sent into exile to Gorky, shortly before the Olympic Games, and still lives there, isolated from his family and friends. In this photo, taken before his exile, he converses with a correspondent from the German Press Agency.

52. The writer Aleksandr Zinoviev with his wife, Olga. Professor of formal logic, Zinoviev had an international reputation in his field and was published widely in foreign scientific journals. Away for a year to give courses at the University of Munich, where he now lives, he was abruptly deprived of his Soviet citizenship. His first novel, *The Yawning Heights,* a scathing satire on Communism, attracted worldwide attention. He has written four since then, the latest recently published in France.

53. Aïda Sichov, with the celebrated priest Dudko, who baptized her when she was thirty. Since then, she has been godmother to many friends' children. Father Dudko, who enjoys wide popularity, was forced by the regime to do a public self-criticism, mostly for the benefit of the foreign press.

Previous double page
54. A great lover of painting, Sichov befriended countless artists of all sorts: "official," "modernist," and "avant-garde." For those denied public exhibits, he would organize showings in his Moscow apartment.

55. Dmitri Plavinsky (left) was one of the first avant-garde painters. His first works, judged completely unacceptable from the standpoint of socialist realism, have never been exhibited. Next to him, Aleksandr Ariefiev, also a veteran of the Soviet avant-garde. He began painting his "decadent" canvases in 1940, when he was seventeen.

56. Anatoly Okorokov, an "official" painter, one of Sichov's closest friends, is widely known for his stunning stained-glass windows designed for museums and public buildings.

57. Alexei Paustorsky, a painter belonging to the "moderate" avant-garde. Son of the famous Soviet writer Constantin Paustorsky, he died from a drug overdose.

58. In his studio, Anatoly Maslov, surrounded by his paintings. Once considered modernist, his paintings now hang in the Leningrad Museum.

59. Dmitri Gordeev is one of the best painters of the younger generation. He has painted portraits of dissident physicists, and participated in the censured exhibition of 1974. Today he is officially recognized and displays his paintings in Moscow.

60. Avtandil Varadze has been called the Glory of Georgia, where he was born. He was one of the first Soviet avant-garde painters to have his canvases displayed at New York's Museum of Modern Art. He died in 1976.

61. The clergyman on the left, Aleksandr Mer, is a Jew who converted to Orthodoxy. He believes that the future of Israel would be much improved if it accepted the Christian religion. Next to him, Father Sergei Zheludkov, one of the countless priests to whom the Soviet regime refuses a church.

62. The historian Roy Medvedev, author of numerous works published in the West, notably in France: *Stalinism, On Socialist Democracy, Was the October Revolution Inevitable?* and, with the collaboration of his twin brother, Zhores, *A Question of Madness*, a book about Zhores's brief stay in a special psychiatric clinic. Roy Medvedev belongs to the neo-Marxist group, and is tolerated by the regime. The publication of his books, however, has not been authorized in the USSR.

63. Svetlana Melnikova, with Vladimir Ossipov, created one of the first *samizdat* papers, *Veche* (*Eternity*). It was not completely underground and the editor provided his name and address. *Eternity* did not last long, and Ossipov found himself in prison.

64. Yuri Orlov was tried for his intervention in favor of Leonid Plyushch, president of a Moscow committee formed to monitor observance of the Helsinki Accords. He was sentenced to twelve years' detention for "anti-Soviet propaganda."

65. Vladimir Ossipov, well-known dissident and Aïda Sichov's first husband, was arrested and condemned to five years of prison for his part in the famous Red Square demonstration against the invasion of Czechoslovakia. After his release from prison, Aïda found him this house in a village; political prisoners may not live in the city during a period of parole equal to their time of detention. Arrested again in 1974, he is currently in prison.

66. Ilya Gazunov. A famous official painter, he has done portraits of the famous, notably the kings of Spain and Sweden. His masterpiece, visible at the left in his studio, is an immense canvas: "The Mystery of the Twentieth Century." It includes world figures ranging from Tsar Nicholas II, Lenin, and even Solzhenitsyn, to Mussolini, Jean-Paul Sartre, and the Pope. Glazunov is struggling with the regime, which doesn't want to accept this painting for any of the state museums.

67. Vyacheslav Illykov is a talented official sculptor whose moderate modernism, influenced by Henry Moore, is tolerated by the censors.

68. Anatoly Zverev, shown here with his family, is one of the first artists of the Soviet avant-garde to have exhibited his work in Paris (1973). The paintings were judged unsuitable by the regime. The historian Andrei Amalrik arranged the showing with the help of his friends, in particular Igor Markevitch. That is one reason, among others, for Amalrik's internment in a *gulag*. Zverev was also threatened, but was finally allowed to go free.

69. Anatoly Shcharansky, accused of treason, which is punishable by death, was held secretly for sixteen months before trial, in 1978. His mother had asked a lawyer, Madame Kaminskaya, to defend him. She accepted. Eleven days later — before the trial — the lawyer was expelled from the Moscow Law College and lost the right to practice. Her husband lost his job, and they were driven from their apartment. Other lawyers refused to be involved. Shcharansky was sentenced to thirteen years in a special camp.

70.   Venedikt Erofeyev, writer, is the author of *Moscow to the End of the Line*, an hilarious epic about an irredeemable drunkard. Quite a drinker himself, his name, also that of a brand of vodka popular before the Revolution, often passes for a pseudonym.

71.   The famous poet Bella Akhmadulina. Married at one time to Yevgeni Yevtushenko, she published her works in the first semiclandestine reviews and journals, like the famous *Syntax*.

72. General Grigorenko was originally a resolute Marxist and Party member until he became disillusioned with Communism. He became a dissident and twice stayed at length in psychiatric institutions. When freed, he was authorized to go to the United States. It was only a trap: he was immediately deprived of his Soviet citizenship.

73. The avant-garde poet Leonid Gubanov is highly talented, but not recognized by the literary bureaucracy. At seventeen, he founded a circle of aspiring poets, which modestly named itself Group of Geniuses.

Previous double page

74. A view of the famous "forbidden exhibition" of September 1974. A large number of painters whose work — called decadent — was refused entrance into official exhibits organized their own open-air exhibit in Moscow. It lasted only an hour and a half. The police arrived very quickly and dispersed the painters and visitors, in some instances using brutality. The site itself was then bulldozed over by the KGB. Almost all of the canvases, however, were saved.

75, 76, 77. The exhibition of Chemiakin's work that Sichov organized in his apartment earned him an unannounced visit from the soldiers, on constant patrol in front of his house. When they rang the bell, Sichov told his wife to open the door; the result is this photograph.

75
76

77

78, 79, 80. Scenes from one of the psychiatric hospitals, scornfully referred to with the diminutive *psikushka.* These "special hospitals" are not run by the Ministry of Health, but rather by the Ministry of the Interior, specifically the KGB.

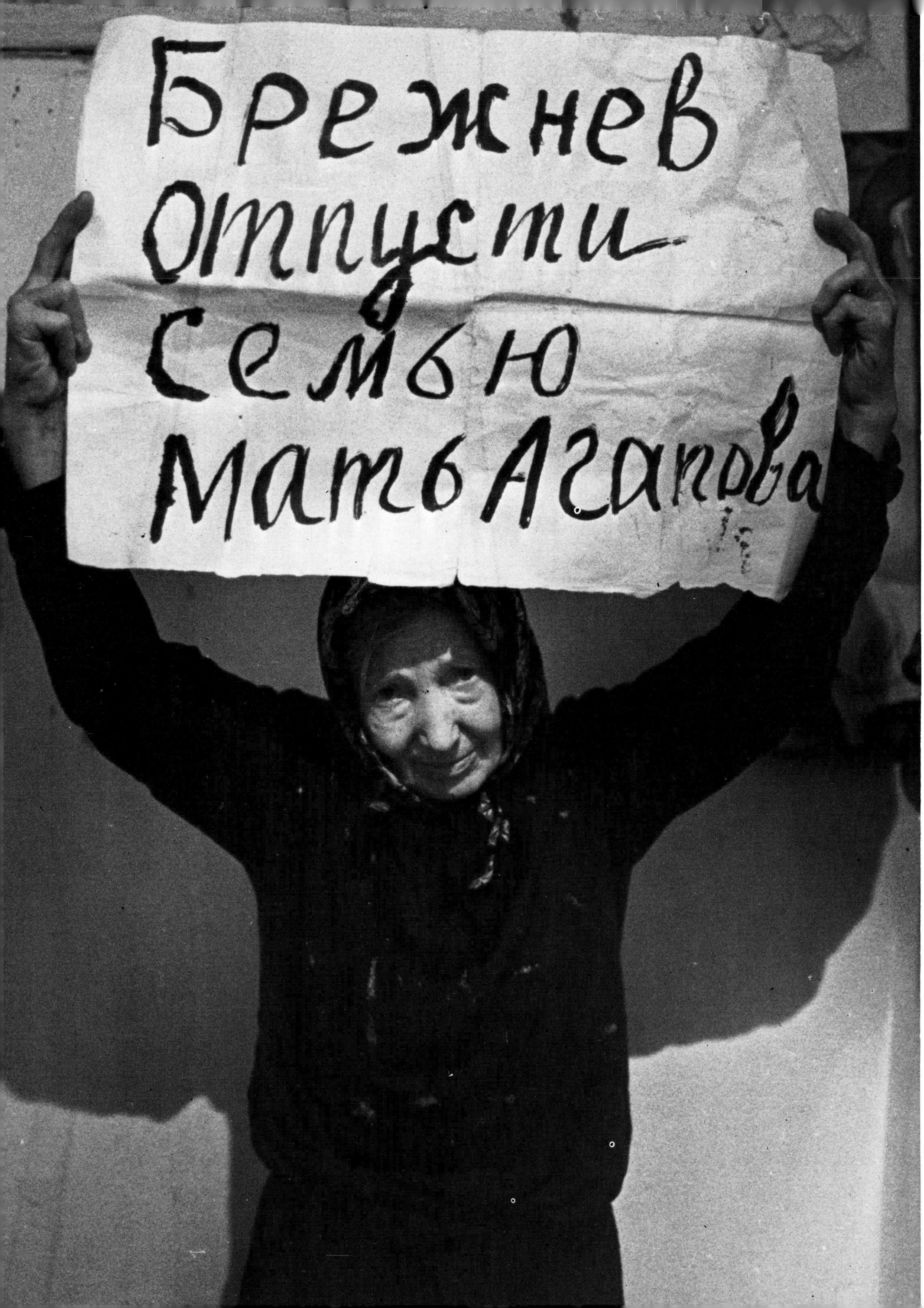

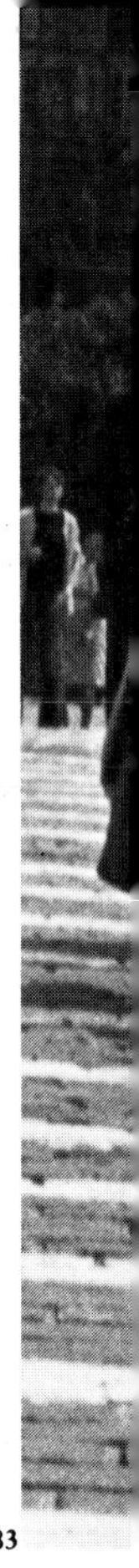

83

84

Previous double page
81. One of the two main synagogues in Moscow, during Yom Kippur, 1975. Sichov had come here with the well-known dissident Shcharansky.

82, 83, 84. The drama of a mother, Antonina Agapova, is told in these three photographs. Her son is in Sweden, but his young wife and small child have had to remain in the USSR. All his wife's requests to join him were denied. On June 15, 1979, Antonina went to Red Square waving a sign which read: "Brezhnev, let the Agapov family leave." Police officers, concentrated at Red Square, quickly intervened: they gagged her and ripped her sign away.

Following double page
85. In addition to those dissidents whose names have become well known, millions deported to the camps die anonymously. In the cemetery at Potma, there are no names on the graves. The numbers here do not even reflect the numbers assigned in the *gulag*; they are simply row numbers.

Chapter 8

Workers Turn to the Black Market to Live Better

Everyone is familiar with Marx's two key precepts: "From each according to his work, to each according to his needs," during the socialist period, then once the final stage of Communism has been reached: "From each according to his abilities, to each according to his needs." Marx, of course, never claimed to forecast a time span for this evolution. For Lenin in 1917, this stage seemed far in the distant future. The most urgent task for the present was to destroy the bourgeoisie and capitalism, then to construct socialism, modestly defined by him as "the power of the Soviet people plus electrification."

Lenin came up against such vast difficulties that he had to lower his expectations. In 1921, he announced the creation of the NEP (New Economic Policy), which was a temporary concession to private enterprise, in that it permitted commercial activities and slowed the pace of agricultural collectivization. The famine in 1921–1922 forced this indirect recognition of the dreaded profit motive. A second famine followed in 1933, and was the most devastating Russia had known, resulting in confirmed cases of cannibalism. One can easily see why Marx's stages were set aside for the moment.

With the relative recovery of the economy, theory regained its charm. The first phase, preliminary to the establishment of socialism, had been accomplished: victory "over capitalism in the cities and the countryside." Encouraged by victory in World War II, Moscow announced that socialism had been achieved in the USSR, then in the satellites. At the Twenty-first Congress, Khrushchev announced that the country would be advancing toward the final stage of Communism after a small intermediate step — catching up with the United States — by 1970. The impetuous Nikita made himself even clearer when he spoke with an Indian publicist. In early 1960, the publicist asked him when the USSR would achieve Communism. Nikita Sergeyevich responded, "We have every reason to believe this goal will be achieved between 1975 and 1980, unless there is a war in the meantime." If it had been only Khrushchev who claimed this, the prediction could have been attributed simply to his usual exuberance. But these terms are very clearly confirmed in the Soviet Communist Party program: Communist society was to be realized in 1980. The last phrase, in capitals, proclaims: "The Party solemnly declares that the present generation of Soviets will live in Communism!" There is no doubt that Communism exists today in the USSR, but the question could be asked if the principle "to each according to his needs . . ." is applied. There is a large difference between the standard of living in the city and that in the country. People living in a large urban area live better than in a small village. The rural exodus is a common phenomenon in every contemporary society, and no matter what the social order, Russian villages would lose population. There is a difference, though, between a Western peasant and a Russian one: the Russian cannot leave the countryside when he wants. For many years, he had no "domestic passport," just as in czarist times he had been attached to the land. He resented this discrimination profoundly. The Bolsheviks always preferred the industrial workers, who would form the base for the badly needed proletariat. Through the 1930s and the times of famine, of forced collectivization and "dekulakization" the peasants were treated as second-class citizens. *Kulaks* were large landowners, as despised as city capitalists, but millions of peasants were proclaimed Kulaks and deported, although their one offense was refusing to give their cows to the *kolkhoz*. In the eyes of the regime, peasants were pariahs, useful only for feeding city workers, despite Lenin's proclamation of the sacred bond between workers and peasants.

THE WORKERS

It is impossible for a Westerner to imagine life in a *kolkhoz,* because nothing here is similar to it. On the other hand, there are only small differences in the industrial domain. Emmanuel Berl used to say that a "socialist" automobile is only a bad capitalist automobile. A Soviet factory is a capitalist factory that functions less well; its productivity is lower and its workers are paid less. Official Soviet sources are full of figures that confirm these three points. Hedrick Smith, for three years the chief of the *New York Times*'s Moscow Bureau, suggested this when he wrote in *The Russians:* "The Soviet economy may rank second to the American in terms of total output, but even by Soviet statistics its output per capita in 1973 ranked 15th, and by American calculations it ranked 25th — behind the United States, Canada, West Germany, France, Britain, all of northern and central Europe, Japan, Australia, New Zealand, several oil-producing Arab states, East Germany and Czechoslovakia." Volumes could be filled with quotations illustrating this from *Pravda* and *Izvestia*. The following passage comes from *Trud* (Work), the organ of the trade unions. It is an editorial concerning the swelling in the number of trained personnel in the factories, despite Party warnings. The article is relatively old, but nothing today has changed.

The Miass equipment-manufacturing company employs 800-odd workers divided into 15 workshops to make files. The management is made up not only of the 15 workshop directors, but also of 19 sections and 50 different offices. Thus, a very ordinary file manufactured by this factory costs its weight in gold to make. Some workshops have no more than five workers, but in addition there are a workshop director, a foreman, a production specialist and a procedures division. The manufacturing division has its own accounting department and is considered to be completely independent, although it manufactures nothing and is unable to do so. Despite this, the 13 workers in this division have as their supervisors: a departmental manager, an office manager, an engineer, and an accountant. There are even areas where there are no workers, simply managers.

This paradox in the very industries that the regime has encouraged — electrification, heavy industry, arms, and now electronics — is one of the most surprising facets of Soviet reality. Manufacturing is meticulously directed; it has been subject to rigorous planning, from threading the smallest machine to the color of material used to make pants (their cut has not changed since before WWII). Simultaneously, industry is completely anarchical. Everyone in the USSR is familiar with the phenomenon of *sturmovchtina,* a word that evokes the image of a charging or a storming by cavalry. The word is now used to describe a constant practice in every branch of industry. One of the first rules of Soviet planning is exaggeration; the socialist economy must always be presented as progressing; every Five-Year Plan must surpass the preceding one by an impressive margin. Underpaid workers do as little as possible, because they feel they are exploited and because they try to compensate for their insufficient salaries by moonlighting, or working "on the left," as the Russians say. This accounts for widespread absenteeism. There are constant work interruptions for reasons other than sickness: arrangements between two co-workers so that one can shop for the other, while the other stays behind and pretends to share the tasks. At the same time, because they are badly paid, workers tend to drag and thus produce less than asked. More must be asked of them to get what is desired. The system of "charging" or "storming" works this way: during periods of production, the workers perform at only half-capacity, but as deadlines approach, the managers and foremen put pressure on them to speed up so they will be able to offer their superiors statistics indicating they have fulfilled the Plan or, better yet, gone beyond it. These figures are given for the most part in terms of production tonnage; all sorts of trickery can take place at this point on the part of the factory managers. A Communist leader severely scolded a factory that manufactures farm equipment for using a heavy alloy in their machinery, simply to meet the norm of the Plan. Hedrick Smith mentions another illustration of this, familiar to any Russian housewife, who checks the assembly date on each appliance before purchasing. To find one which will be likely to work, dates immediately following payday must be avoided, since alcoholism and fatigue automatically ruin a certain percentage of the products, and as for those appliances manufactured during the last ten days of the month, they are hastily thrown together in order for the factory to meet the Plan's quotas.

SOVIET SALARIES

The state of Soviet industry is a result of any number of factors, but the main cause is insufficient salaries at every level of Soviet society except for a minority, known as the *nomenklatura,* a term just beginning to be recognized because of Michael Voslensky's book. Synonym for the "new class," which Milovan Djilas, Tito's right-hand man, described in the 1950s, the Soviet *nomenklatura* is the list of high party officials who hold power. According to Voslensky, this list includes 1.5 percent of the country's total population: that is, 750,000 families or 3,000,000 people. This must be taken into consideration before discussing the average Soviet pay. Soviet society seems to be the most inequitable on earth when comparisons are made between the material situation of Soviet workers, employees, engineers, doctors, and members of the *nomenklatura*. No actual measure of comparison is possible, because differences in salaries or appointments do not describe the difference in the quality of life each class can afford. The *nomenklatura* enjoy privileges and have access to services that cannot be bought by others in the society: free *dachas*, party cars, vacations in luxury resorts run by the Party, etcetera. They also have a floor, called Section 100, reserved for them in the GUM department store; no ordinary citizen has access, even if he has made millions on the black market.

As for the rest of the population, it is important to remember that Russian salaries converted to Western currency seem ridiculously low. The ruble can be exchanged only in Switzerland, whose conversion rate is artificially high. The lowest salary comes to 60 rubles, about $94 a month; 120 rubles — $187 — is considered a good average salary. Higher salaries are received by correspondingly fewer people. Actual workers are relatively well paid and earn 120 rubles, even 200 ($312.50). Remember, there is no way to compare this world with the West in absolute terms. There are methods that can be used to determine the amount of working time necessary to purchase a certain product, which can bring us closer to a real comparison. The same work time is required for monthly rent as for a pair of shoes. Two months' rent equals a pair of pants; for foreign jeans, you would have to pay eight to ten months' rent. But even another system of comparison is not satisfactory: the market-basket method. it is not useful to compare work time with a pound of meat; first, because meat is very hard to come by in the Soviet Union. When there is some to buy, it is of mediocre quality, hacked up and always sold with the bone (even when it is a "boneless" piece, a corresponding weight is added in). Moreover, the Russians are used to eating much less meat: even if it is more expensive than in the United States, it does not have the same effect proportionally on a Soviet housewife's budget. Nonetheless, the most important reason

why it is difficult to compare salaries, buying power, and the price of products is the complete difference in lifestyles. In contrast to the West, foodstuffs are relatively less expensive than manufactured products. A pair of pants equals two months' rent, but a countless number of Soviet citizens have only two pairs, one for summer, the other for winter. They may have a third for special occasions. Clothing is used until it is completely worn out. Men rarely have more than one sweater, which normally lasts two to three years. The easiest way to conjure up an image is to think of France during World War II. This offers a more concrete picture than comparing statistics. I can propose a statistical comparison, however, if necessary. I created it from a variety of sources and impressions; I asked a large number of people who had come from the East with a fair knowledge of the West. The average salaried employee, whatever his occupation, including professionals (not including those dependent on artistic talent or athletic prowess), has a third, even a fourth, of the buying power of a corresponding Westerner.

For workers, this entails other aspects. It is true that there is virtually no unemployment in the USSR. There could not be, because work is required. Unemployment, in fact, is illegal and punishable as "parasitism" if proven. Everyone is placed in the occupation for which he is prepared. Consequently, there are usually three times the number who are truly necessary for a specific job. They are paid a third as much, using a seemingly justifiable logic. This system thus makes universally guaranteed employment result in equality for the great majority of Soviet people. On the salary scale, there are many fewer intermediary categories than in the West. More simply, there is equality of misery.

ALCOHOLISM

The incredible new outbreak of alcoholism in the USSR is not wholly attributable to Communism or to the confusion it engenders. There always has been drinking in Russia. Rotgut was illegally distilled by the peasants and called *samogon* under Nicholas II, and probably even long before him. In Moscow, the French expression "drunk as a Pole" (and not "drunk as a Russian") would probably seem like unfair discrimination. It is a national proclivity, due probably to certain living conditions and a particular environment. Some feel that the Slavic soul needs to quench its thirst for the absolute, or fulfill its propensity for melancholy through alcohol. This said, it is undeniable that alcoholism has reached alarming proportions in the USSR today. Anyone who has studied the Soviet Union agrees, and the fact is openly admitted by the Soviets themselves in the official press. More and more foreign visitors, since the USSR has opened its borders to travelers, bring back stories of the countless people they have seen leaning on lampposts and against trees, from early morning on. As the police approach they stiffen up to feign sobriety. According to an unwritten law, as long as a drunkard is upright, he is not carted off to the nearest station. The only ones eligible for this are those who cannot stand upright, who are lying on benches or stretched out on the sidewalk.

There is an unexpectedly kindhearted attitude toward alcoholism and especially toward drunkeness, in the Soviet Union.

In the first place, any and all contact with the militia is feared by the populace, because these cops, wearing red-bordered caps, never miss a pretext for handing out tickets when not specifically arresting someone. A jaywalker crossing against the light can be fined as much as 10 rubles ($15.63). The drunkard who has been picked up and brought to the station by a policeman will calmly sleep off his alcohol overnight, and be released the following morning without paying a kopeck. The writer Viktor Nekrasov, now living in Paris, who received the Stalin Award for his book on the war, is inexhaustible on this subject, one that reveals his nostalgia for Russian life. In his book *Notes of a Wanderer,* he consecrates a humorous and touching chapter to Muscovite drinkers. On certain days (usually semimonthly paydays), groups of men, by twos or threes, gather in front of the rare government specialty shops. Vodka comes in liter bottles, so they share. The store opens at 11 A.M., but they begin waiting at 9. Once they have their precious bottle safely in hand, in order not to lose a minute the happy consumers head for a small square or neighborhood park. A *babushka* (an old grandmother) has usually set up long wooden tables. Standing, they empty the bottles, eating cooked potatoes already prepared for a few kopecks by the old lady. The arrival of the inevitable policeman is described in kind, even gentle, terms. Full of understanding, which clashes with his habitual brusque tone, he comes closer and asks the citizens to disperse, explaining that there is ordinarily no eating or drinking or transacting of business permitted in public places. This first request has no effect. The cop's voice becomes persuasive and friendly, and he refers to the "cultured" nature of the drinkers, who should understand that the place is not one for drinking. (Words like *cultivated* or *cultured* are over- and misused frequently in the USSR: in restaurants, "cultured" service is advertised, a "cultured" attitude is recommended to salespersons in shops, etcetera.)

The Soviets do not simply indulge drunks. A friendly attitude exists; it could even be said that they are loved. (This attitude is in complete contrast to the way drug addicts are treated. They are ruthlessly pursued and punished.) Sichov recalled the case of a decadent, lazy nonconformist painter friend of his. At the Painters' Union, he was at first refused a small stipend to help him survive, but as soon as Sichov commented, "But what do you want him to do? He's just a poor drunkard . . . ," the officials' expressions softened: his case became worthy of attention and they helped him. Sichov added that the fact that he drinks nothing at all sometimes became a serious handicap for him in his profession, particularly in dealing with the administration. While discussing business, or considering a particular transaction, a bottle was often present. "If I refused to drink," said Sichov, "I spoiled the mood and immediately became a suspicious character."

The explanation that this general attitude is grounded in humanitarian feelings is not shared by all dissidents nor by all analysts of the Soviet economy. The dissidents feel that the rise in alcoholism is directly related to the regime's unwillingness to suppress it, and in fact, believe that the regime encourages it. As proof, they maintain that the day before payday the kiosks are stuffed with extra bottles of vodka at inflated prices, and not beer and wine (a much better buy). As with everything else, expectations must be met and production must automatically increase with each Five-Year Plan. The warehouse foreman must also meet the official quotas and turn in a sales record. A good number of people, however, take the more cynical view that the regime encourages alcoholism because alcoholism diffuses discontent before it can become violence.

Previous double page
86. This line formed quickly with the announcement of a newly arrived selection of imported dresses. The quality, mediocre by our standards, does not justify the 80 ruble price tag, which is equivalent to a beginning engineer's monthly salary.

87. Store windows were not always so well stocked in this old woman's lifetime, as she probably remembers the famine years that followed the Revolution. Russian women never go out without a shopping bag, in case they come across a store where a line has formed because some coveted consumer goods have just arrived.

88. Inside Passage, a large Moscow department store. The crowds are always this dense because shoppers stream by the thousands from the less well supplied provinces.

89. This old woman digging through her coin purse has a rather unusual occupation for a socialist country: shoeshine. This is an occupation she shares with the Kurds, who hold a virtual monopoly over the trade.

90. Red Square and the Kremlin. As in front of Saint Mark's in Venice, a photographer takes souvenir portraits for the countless tourists who have traveled here from the provinces.

Previous double page

91.   There is a permanent housing shortage in Moscow, where everyone wants to live. These notice-covered walls have been named the "Lodging Exchange"; shares and exchanges are proposed.

92.   In Moscow's famous subway, underneath the gold archway and leaning against a marble wall, a man dozes off, his grandson in his arms.

93.   Again the "Lodging Exchange," in Moscow. These old women will have little success in finding the modest accommodations they desire.

Previous double-pages
94. Russia has always had cripples. In the distant past, when infirmities were considered trials from heaven, no one paid them much attention. This man scorns prostheses, though his benefits would pay for them; he is apparently resigned to his lot, which doesn't seem to concern the passersby.

95. These wooden houses made up a picturesque neighborhood of old Moscow. The whole street was razed to make way for the Olympic Games.

96. The retired abound in the public parks of provincial cities, as here in Kazan. Retirement comes early in the Soviet Union: for men at sixty, for women at fifty, and a good number of salaried workers can retire after the age of fifty. In the military, early retirement is practically the rule, except for officers of high rank.

97. Moscow, 1972. A young woman is writing, in chalk, a poem praising Stalin. This unusual activity is a lot easier because there are no passersby. This deserted street is closely watched by the police: the large square building houses an innocent-sounding agency, the Ministry of Intermediate Industry, which like many others actually supplies the military.

98. The Moscow Bird Market. At the *Ptitzy Yarmark,* the "bird fair," all sorts of small animals can also be found: dogs, fish, even small monkeys. Right after the Revolution, when food for animals was scarce, owning a pet dog signified membership in the old bourgeoisie. Today again, many families own them.

Following double page
99. Summer in Moscow. Games of chess and dominoes spring up in parks surrounding the capitol at the first signs of fair weather.

Previous double page 100. In the Georgian capital, once more called Tbilisi in its own tongue, these old women remain unchanged. The young Komsomol members are probably unaware that the city was founded in the fifth century and fought over by Byzantines, Persians, and Arabs.

101, 102, 103, 104. Soviet people spend time in the public gardens for different reasons. Some are simply vagrants, as in all large cities. Others have money: they are merchants from the southern republics who have come to sell agricultural products that are scarce and in demand in the cities: oranges, watermelons, and cantaloupe. They must wait in public for the departure of their plane, because hotels never have vacancies.

101

102

Previous double page
105. Two drunks have just fallen over in one of Moscow's streets, after a scuffle. A van from the militia (uniformed police) will pick them up and bring them to the station.

106, 107. Encountered in a Suzdal courtyard, this threatening man finally let Sichov photograph him shirtless.

108. An alcoholic has just collapsed in a Moscow street. This common event arouses only a glance from the inhabitants.

109. In Kazan, beggars like this invalid exist despite official prohibition of soliciting in the USSR. It is considered a holdover from the capitalist past.

Following double page
110. Alcoholism is endemic to large cities throughout the USSR. This scene is in Vladimir, a city close to Moscow which Ivan the Terrible wanted to make his capital. He had even had a kremlin, now in ruins, constructed there.

Chapter 9

The Peasants Put All Their Effort into Their Own Private Allotments

The Western press's nickname for Khrushchev, "Mr. Corn," was more a reference to the failures of this major Soviet crop than an indication of its abundance. Nikita Sergeyevich gave at least twenty-five major speeches during his career and over half dealt with farming and agriculture. This was, perhaps, because of his rural origins, but it is significant that when Leonid Brezhnev replaced him, Brezhnev's first order of business was to convene a special council on agricultural problems. The new Party secretary settled for a thirty-five-page report that was enough to illustrate a rather significant failure: during the five previous years, total agricultural production had increased by only 1 percent. Worse, in 1965 the total for the more important products (flax being an exception) had not yet reached the pre–World War II level. Stuffed with quotations from Lenin, this report ended with a couplet dedicated to the Soviet citizen, member of the Communist Party, who had been the first man sent into space. The chasm between that Soviet performance and the state of its agriculture was demonstrated that same year when the USSR took its second massive delivery of foreign, especially American, wheat.

Agriculture has been the Achilles' heel of every Soviet Five-Year Plan. Each Plan, from the first in 1926 to the latest, 1975–1980, has announced with great fanfare the constant improvement in the quality of life. The disparity between rhetoric and reality has always been most obvious when one considered agriculture. The first Plan covered a period that ended in 1934. According to an analyst of the Soviet economy, Alec Nove, "The year 1933 was the lowest point of the dizziest decline in the standard of living in peacetime." That did not stop Stalin from declaring, in January of the same year, "We have undoubtedly reached the point where material conditions for the workers and the peasants will steadily improve from year to year. The only ones who refuse to see this are the sworn enemies of the Soviet regime. . . ." He went one better in 1935: "Life has become better, comrades; life has become more joyful." The last American wheat deliveries in 1975–1976 were significant for their size: the first installment was 8,000,000 tons. The total price for these imports was $1,800,000,000. The government bureau in charge of this operation was called, ironically, Khlebexport, a name that means "the expor-

tation of bread." The word harks back to the time when czarist Russia exported grain, and the Ukraine, Khrushchev's and Brezhnev's homeland, was known as the "breadbasket of Europe." Today, any exports go to specific socialist countries, for political reasons. Another export made "for political reasons" should be mentioned in passing: Stalin delivered 1,000,000 tons of grain to Hitler in 1940; the Germans thus completed their stocks in readiness for the war — against Russia, the following year.

Comparisons have often been made between the two most powerful economies in the world. The USSR has 50 percent more arable land than the United States. Less then 4.5 percent of the American population works in agriculture as against 31 percent in the USSR. In concrete terms, this means that one American farmer feeds 58 of his fellow citizens, while a Russian peasant feeds only 8 of his. This is all the more surprising given the amount of talk one hears in the USSR about increasing farm production. Agriculture has been collectivized, modernized, mechanized, supplied with chemical fertilizers, and provided with vast numbers of tractors and machines. This equipment supply, of course, has been inflated, on paper, by reducing each tractor unit to 15 horsepower, providing a large number for the annual statistics. The praises of agriculture are sung in poetry, and the literature of "socialist realism" is full of enthusiastic agronomist heroes who marry, in the end, apple-cheeked women with wide smiles and scarlet neckerchiefs — who drive tractors.

The results of this epic can be very simply summed up: all these efforts have resulted in the lowest per-acre production of all the Eastern European Communist countries, which, in turn, produce less than the agrarian ones of the West. Some of the multiple and complex causes can be mentioned briefly. Although the Soviet industrial worker performs in an unsatisfactory way, the farmer in a *kolkhoz* shows even less interest in production. In contrast to the worker, the peasant does not receive an hourly wage. His pay is calculated according to the *trudoden*, the workday, the type of labor, the machines used, etcetera. In certain regions the scale is higher, as in the Kazakh. The *trudoden* can be as high as eight times the national average. This calculation does not provide for the vagaries of the weather since in the end a farmer is judged by his results. His pay could be considerably reduced because the quotas are not met. To all of these possible complications another is added: the determination of what part of the *kolkhoz* farmer's produce he himself may keep as payment in kind. In the conditions of scarcity that exist in the USSR, this is the most valuable part of his pay, because the *kolkhoz* farmer can freely sell this produce on the special market known as the *kolkhoz* market. This, then, leads us into another corridor of the seemingly endless agricultural bureaucracy. Without counting the black market, there are two operating markets, which command very different prices for the same products. The government market is supplied by "obligatory deliveries" that *kolkhoz* farmers must make to certain collection areas at prices so low that they hardly cover transportation. In Stalin's time, all produce had to be turned over to the state; whoever tried to get around the system ended up in the *gulag*. There is an ode from this period to the grain convoys, slowly advancing toward the collection area. The poem is called "The Caravan of Peace." The disastrous failure of collective farming has forced the regime to concede two important points: recognition of private plots of land, and payment in kind. The part of the crop a farmer retains can be sold at the *kolkhoz* markets at "free" prices, which are much higher than those at the state markets (though below the black market). Widely documented, these *kolkhoz* markets seem to be the Soviet housewife's principal source of food. She cannot plan meals before she sees what is available, and the *kolkhoz* market is the only dependable source. Even in restaurants, only a rare few of the dishes (of the impressive number on the menu) are made from fresh produce or meat brought from that day's market. The other results of weaknesses in the system are mentioned in the regime's own press stories: an oversized administration, worn-out farming equipment, a chronic lack of spare parts that can put whole storage lots of machines and tractors out of commission. One fact attracts particularly harsh criticism: the constant practice of feeding cattle not only with wheat (paid for in dollars), but also with bread. This has become common procedure for a very simple reason: meat can be sold at a high price in the *kolkhoz* market. A farmer's cattle must be well nourished. The Soviet agricultural situation at times seems so absurd that the sincerity of their efforts must be questioned. For a regime that has developed a space program and created an extremely sophisticated arms industry, is agriculture simply made subordinate to the rest? The housewife's supplies are the least of its concerns, now that the serious scarcity is past. The regime can buy its grain from foreign countries, like the rest of the industrialized world. Thus, not only do American farmers indirectly support the Soviet arms industry; the American taxpayer actively participates in it because, in order to sell its own farmers' grain on the world market, America has subsidized the industry. Here, the West's absurdity meets and surpasses the Kremlin's.

The failure of collectivization can be easily grasped through a comparison, summed up in a few figures. In all Soviet-bloc countries, the regimes have allowed small "personal" plots of land (they wanted to avoid at all cost the term *private*, a word that suggests "property," "owning," and so on). From these handkerchief-sized plots — in the USSR they do not even amount to 1.3 percent of all cultivated land — the peasants manage to furnish the essential foodstuffs for the country: 30 percent of the milk, meat, and vegetables, 34 percent of the eggs, and 61 percent of the potatoes, according to 1978 figures, the last available. These percentages were much higher in the past. The fact that they have decreased does not mean that collective farming has succeeded better but rather that the area of individual plots has steadily been reduced by the regime. After all, this provisionary concession to private enterprise was first made in the 1920s. The success of these private plots — which even Khrushchev dared not abolish — suggests that the practically permanent crisis in Soviet agriculture can be largely attributed to collectivization and to its bureaucratic methods.

Previous double page

111. The historic city of Suzdal, cradle of ancient Muscovy, possessed 36 churches. All except one have been secularized and converted to depots or other official buildings. In the foreground is one of the tiny parcels of land left to the peasants. These farmers produce 30 percent of the principle foodstuffs, despite the fact that these small farming areas represent only 1.3 percent of all arable land.

112. The famous cupolas of the sixteenth-century Suzdal cathedral, which was transformed into a museum by the Bolsheviks. In the foreground, again, one of the individual lots that are lovingly farmed by their peasant owners. This small-scale agriculture produces the eggs, meat, vegetables, and fresh fruit that Soviet housewives find in the open market.

Previous double page
113. The choice is very meager at this market: a calf's head and feet, a slice of pumpkin. One of the sellers is screaming at Sichov because she saw him taking photographs.

114. On the outskirts of the city, life has not changed since Yuri Dolgoruki founded the Rostov-Suzdal principality, which was the forerunner of the principality of Moscow.

115. Despite collective farming, the peasant's daily life remains very much as it has always been. These *kolkhoz* farmers are serving tea from the traditional samovar of their ancestors.

116. Behind this primitive house lies a pile of firewood. It will go into an enormous tiled stove that has a wide, flat top: a warm place to sleep.

117. This *kolkhoz* family poses in front of their *izba* (village house).

118. These men are dressed for work, with quilted coats to protect them against hard Russian winters, when the thermometer dips below −30°C.

Following double page
119. Inside an *izba*. The children lie warm in bed on top of the large tile stove. In the past, farm animals used to spend winter nights in these houses. Today, the practice is prohibited by law.

115

117

116

118

Chapter 10

They Have Not Been Able to Abolish Christmas

Only estimates on the number of the devout can be obtained, and even these figures must be used with care. There are no official statistics, because the USSR is an atheist state. The Church's own estimates, when drawn from actual baptism or marriage certificates and not just extrapolated from a few scattered figures, are also hard to count on, because a baptism celebrated by church-going parents does not guarantee that their child will continue to be a believer. Baptism could also be simply an outward manifestation of a certain attachment to tradition, and not necessarily an expression of spiritual devotion. Figures vary widely. An Irish journalist spoke of 80,000,000 regular churchgoers, but this figure is obviously too high. Metropolitan Nikolai Krutitzy intimated to an American group that there were several tens of millions in the USSR. When asked if there might be 50,000,000 faithful, he responded in the affirmative. The Catholic and Protestant minorities have been carefully counted by their respective clergy. There seem to be 3,000,000 Protestant Baptists, the largest minority group. The tallying of Jews is a little different, though the problem is similar to that of Orthodoxy. There are many people, even young ones, who attend services on major traditional holidays, but who are not really believers.

Those who attend church without being true believers fall into two categories: they either go to church for the sake of tradition (Orthodox ceremonies on the important holidays, especially Easter, are extremely beautiful and inspiring), or they attend church as a form of protest. Since there has been no direct persecution of churchgoers since the 1950s, the Church can also be for them a weekly meeting place of friends against the regime. It is a means for expressing discontent without being an active resister.

There has been a significant evolution in the regime's attitude toward the faithful. In the first years of "revolutionary furor," the Bolsheviks severely attacked the Church. A considerable but unknown number of priests, including high prelates, lost their lives. They were considered, like many other groups of citizens, counter-revolutionary or adversaries of socialism. Churches were gutted and oftentimes transformed into granaries. This violence intimidated believers to such an extent that they no longer dared practice openly. There were many who kept a small corner of their bedroom sacred: icons were lit by candles and preserved. Some, like Aleksandr Zinoviev's elderly mother, added Stalin's photograph. An enormous change in attitude took place during World War II, when Stalin, terrified by the rapid progress of Hitler's invasion, tried to inspire the population to action by recognizing the Orthodox Church and the patriotic and military traditions of the czarist past. Bishops could be seen blessing Red Army battalions on their way to war. But even before this time, certain concessions had been tacitly granted. Two important religious holidays, Christmas and Easter, had been authorized, although this did not mean that the regime ever stopped preaching against materialism. Atheism and antireligious propaganda had been institutionalized, and Christmas was a workday like any other. Rather, it was different only in the sense that Party organizations and the Komsomol loaded on extra work during the holidays, or else invited the workers to special after-hours ideological discussions. Christmas trees appeared in many stores, however, and small candles and ornaments became available for decoration. The subtlety was in beginning to sell the trees not for Christmas but for New Year's Day, an official holiday. There remained the problem of Father Christmas, however, another survival from religious superstition. The propaganda machine (the Agitprop) quickly found a secular significance, with a name that simply evoked winter's arrival. Father Christmas became "Grandfather Frost," and was divested of any mystical significance. The regime recognized its limitations: "consciousness-raising groups" on Party line, Marxist-Leninist classes and *diamat* couldn't replace hallowed feast-days and celebrations. Every attempt to replace the traditional religious celebrations with new laicized or civil holidays has failed. Minimally decorating the marriage bureaus has not turned the cold formality of an administrative marriage into a church wedding.

Where does religion stand today? Vladimir Sichov's views are noteworthy, since they come from his own personal experiences and travels. He visited countless churches and attended many services in the most important orthodox monasteries — in order to photograph them. Also, his wife, Aïda, recently became converted and was baptized by the famous Father Dmitri Dudko. Since then, she has had not only her own children, but many friends' children, baptized.

Not everyone agrees about the Church's present situation. Some dissidents feel that it is worsening, while others think that conditions are slowly improving. Gleb Tikhonin, one of the founders of the Committee for the Defense of the Faithful, maintains that there are 10,000,000 Orthodox believers who regularly attend church, while Father Dudko, on the other hand, thinks the figure is closer to 30,000,000. Unlike Tikhonin, he believes from his own experience that more and more people are turning toward the Church, which seems to be true.

"What I saw in the churches," says Sichov, "happens not only during holy days, but also on ordinary days, . . . anywhere you go. On days set aside for baptism there will be thirty newborn babies brought by their parents. This is all the more significant because today in order to be baptized or to have your children baptized you have to show your passport [a special ID called a 'domestic passport']. You must register your whole family, and one never knows whether there will be unpleasant consequences. Several years in a row, I visited the Pechory monastery at Pskov, and the Zagorsk monastery two or three times a year and saw as many as twenty thousand people at Pskov, sometimes thirty thousand. Religious holidays in the USSR are, of course, still workdays. I always wondered what made these people flock to the churches: they all had been born and raised under the most strictly atheist regime. Most of them were women, but they also went through the Komsomol; they grew up during the Stalin era."

Generally, the reason given for this religious resurgence — or simply attendance — is a profound discouragement, especially among the young people. For decades the propaganda has continually told them to be patient, to accept sacrifices so that in the not too distant future they might arrive at a plateau where everyone will have what they need: paradise, in other words. People have lived a very hard life, especially in the small towns and villages, where they have worked for practically nothing. This generation has not seen a normal life, to say nothing of paradise. They have turned toward religion for hope and consolation.

Since the years 1974–1975, a change has crept over the land: young people have begun to frequent seminary-like institutions to receive religious instruction. Father Ogorodnikov organized these and, of course, was arrested for doing so. These seminaries teach questions of faith and the philosophy of religion rather than Church history or catechism. Ogorodnikov was first sentenced for parasitism (tuneyadstvo). Once inside the camp, he was tried again and sentenced to seven years.

Another phenomenon is emerging among the people: sectarianism. Many of these sects are illegal, like the Baptists, and Pentecostals, or Jehovah's Witnesses. "I attended Baptist meetings in Moscow," continues Sichov, "just as I had visited the synagogues and mosques of Central Asia, or Catholic churches. These sects attract many of the ordinary people. Especially the Baptists, because during their meetings people do not really pray; no one crosses himself. They sing, someone climbs to the pulpit and speaks, but everyone is free to be himself." There, as elsewhere, ritual is absent, but the emotion remains. The regime's attitude toward the Church shows more than a simple toning down of persecution. Oversimplifying greatly, one could say that the Party continues basically to favor uncompromising atheism. But, at the same time, since it has accepted other traditions initially ridiculed by the Bolsheviks, it must ease up similarly on the Orthodox Church. In addition, the regime has accepted, for reasons of artistic propaganda and, simply, tourism, to make and distribute thousands of records of liturgical chants. It has likewise cleaned the icons in the larger churches and monasteries, now objects of close study by researchers from art institutes and academies of history.

Previous double page

120. In the USSR, practicing Orthodox churchgoers are twice as numerous as Communist Party members. This picture was taken on the Feast of the Assumption, at the famous Pechory monastery near Pskov, where thirty thousand had come to worship. In spite of sixty years of anti-religious propaganda, the people have conserved their faith.

121. Covered with icons and religious objects, a *zhurodivy* is a traditional figure. The *zhurodivy* usually possesses a simplicity of spirit and is respected by the peasants because they believe that God protects him. An innocent, he speaks the truth, even to officials.

122. On a trip to the Pechory monastery, this peasant woman brings along with her an icon that normally hangs on her wall, illuminated by candles which are never allowed to go out.

123, 124. In the Pechory monastery, the monks have never interrupted their bell-ringing, even during the Revolution, when countless priests and monks were either assassinated or taken to the first prison camps created by Lenin.

Previous double page
125. The patriarch Pimen, in ceremonial robes, performs the service for the feast of Saint Sergei, who founded the Zagorsk monastery in the fourteenth century.

126, 127, 128. The Pechory Monastery outside Pskov, one of the oldest in Russia, has been the focus of Orthodoxy for more than five hundred years. For the celebration of the anniversary of its founding, tens of thousands of pilgrims, young and old, came to attend the solemnities.

129. As at Lourdes, this invalid is brought less in hopes of a miraculous cure than to seek consolation in meditation.

130. To come to Pskov and Pechory, these peasants dressed up in their finest attire. Their multicolored scarves lend a festive tone.

131. At the Zagorsk monastery, this young priest murmurs a prayer while crossing himself in the Orthodox manner, from left to right.

Following double page
132. This service at Pechory is celebrated by one of Russia's most popular priests, Aleksandr Ogorodnikov. He has been arrested for having organized religious instruction classes for the young. In the past few years, such groups have been multiplying despite the law that prohibits priests from preaching religion outside their churches. The monk seen on the extreme right of the photograph has also been arrested. He is Ogorodnikov's brother.